CAROLYN RESNICK BLOG COLLECTION

Volume One

May 2008 – April 2009

Equine training can be a hazardous activity which may result in serious injury and/or death. Carolyn Resnick and her associates make no warranty or representation and assume neither liability nor responsibility to any person or entity with respect to any loss or damage caused or allegedly caused directly or indirectly by information contained in this book.

Published by:
Carolyn Resnick Method™
2400 Summit Drive
Escondido
CA 92025

www.CarolynResnickBlog.com
www.DanceWithHorses.com

First printing, October 2009

Printed in the USA

Cover Design by Teresa Wood-Woolard

ISBN: 978-1-61623-888-9

ACKNOWLEDGEMENT

I have made so many friends through my work and the blog. So many people to thank. Thank you Stina for your constant development with your horses using my Method. I hope all travelers get to visit your horse programs in the jungle with your wild herd. Thank you Shelly Martin for continuing my Method with Panadero. Shelly is now riding bridless without a neck rope, and I could not be more proud. Thank you to Lisa Zarcades for all you have done to bring awareness to a better way to connect with horses through Panadero and your work with Shelly and myself.

I am over the loss of my 35 year old horse, Stoney. It has been more than a year since he was put down from colic. Lad, Cat and Marchador are all fine and are looking forward to teaching more people my Method.

Thank you to Stormy May for including me on your DVD *'The Path of the Horse'*. Your journey will bring many people back to the real connection and wisdom that horses have to share with us humans. Robin, thank you for the DVD of your work with my Method, sharing your poetry, our long conversations and for loving horses. Thank you Kris for your book of photos and Haiku and all you have done for me. Kemo is still in my heart.

Thank you to Linda Kohanov for her book *'Way of the Horse'*. Thank you to Liz Mitten Ryan for your paintings, your visits, your love of my Method and having a center for people to come to in order to really connect with nature and the equine spirit. Also a double thank you for all the business you have sent to me. Everyone has to see her bull Wooly Bully, his liberty work is charming! Thank you for all the people who have taken private clinics with me and a special thank you to Joy for coming all the way from Denmark. I miss you all a lot!

My life is blessed from all the people in my life and the horses that love them. Mark, thank you for making my blog possible and enabling people to find out about the true nature of horses and how to bring more purpose and meaning to their lives. Thank you Elke for wanting more for the horse world, I am looking forward to your visit. A big thank you to Alessandra Deerinck, my apprentice student. I know that I have the best apprentice a mentor could have. We are best friends and she fills in at any level without me having to say a word.

Thank you, Tally. Tally does everything and anything from script writing to filming, to horse care and running the office. What I like best is how much she loves my viewpoint of connection and the Method and the fun we have on the road and in nature with wild horses. We have been friend for years. Thank you to Jeanette for your friendship and doing all the shipping and being a close friend.

Thanks to Debra Saum for the painting of Marchador and our time together talking about the connection we feel for our guys. Stuart, give all your camels a big kiss from me. Thank you for the book of green drinks. I am drinking them and loving it. Yes, there is a difference, I do feel better.

Last December I took on a new dressage student. I think she came to me because I asked for one from my heart. I was looking for a student that was a gifted dressage rider and then Stacy appeared. She sits on a horse better than I have ever seen a person sit, she has had no training in dressage and she loves my Method and will be working with me over the next year. I will keep you abreast of our progress.

Lastly, thank you to Julia Felton for compiling this collection of blogs into a book and putting it into an easy to use reference format for all my students.

For further information on the Carolyn Resnick Method™ please visit my websites at www.CarolynResnickBlog.com or www.DancewithHorses.com.

TABLE OF CONTENTS

CHAPTER ONE
CAROLYN RESNICK FUNDAMENTALS

TRAINING PHILOSOPHY

The Carolyn Resnick Equestrian Training Method

I was asked the other day if I could sum up what my Method, DVDs and courses are all about and what makes me different to other horse trainers. So I sat down and tried to condense my philosophy into a few sentences, which wasn't so easy! Anyway, please find below what I wrote, I hope it resonates with you.

For those of you who don't know me, you can read a brief biography of me at www.dancewithhorses.com. Of course, for a full story about my younger life with horses and particularly about my education under the tutelage of a herd of wild horses, you should read my book *Naked Liberty*, it's really good! The tag line for the Method I have developed is: *The Foundation for all Equestrian Pursuits*. My focus is on horse training and communication with horses to develop better leadership skills. In time I would like to develop a horsemanship school in my Method. It would be a school of 1-day, 3-day, weekly, monthly and yearly programs in getting back to nature, meditation, art, poetry, music, photography, reading, writing, history, all on the subject of horses as well as dressage and bridleless riding.

My Method has two purposes. One is to empower you to have better relationships in life, both human and equine, based on what you learn from horses. The other purpose is to bring horses and humans together in harmony through a connection built on friendship and respect.

My focus is to deepen your understanding of the horse's mind. You will learn when to allow your horse to shape your leadership to suit his nature, and when to not give in. I show you how to win a horse's respect and how to keep a horse interested in learning and performing, and how to create a perfect connection with him on a daily basis.

The communication I use is body language; talking, sounds of tonality, bonding moments, telepathic messages and leading a horse at the moment the horse is willing to follow. A large part of my course is teaching people how to develop willingness in horses. The tack used for my program is a light reed that cannot hurt the horse and a large area so the horse can escape a student's influence, if he chooses. This is very valuable because it points out to people when their leadership is not appropriate. I believe it is important to stop training when the horse says no.

The neat thing about horses is they are animals that seek companionship, and they will return more willing if they have not been forced. If the horse is not willing at any point, we change the subject and work on something he would enjoy doing. Little by little the horse will do the thing that he refused to do earlier.

One can almost say that my course is one of personal, spiritual growth because the course teaches leadership, which in turn draws horses to you. You learn how to shape the character of the horse to bond and fit in harmony with you in the same way he bonds with other horses. It is a two-way street; you learn how to shape your leadership, to be inviting rather than dominant or persistent, and the horse learns respect and enjoys following your leadership.

I believe that the formula and application of my Method should also be the way we educate our children in school. That is the primary reason I developed my Method; and of course, to train horses in an enjoyable way for the horse. Most other methods are only interested in not abusing the horse. They do not work on the connection or make the training experience for the horse life enhancing. My Method does, and that is the message I would like to spread.

My Logo and My Method

What draws horses and humans together in harmony is a desire for connection, not pressure. This is what my logo means to me. I want to bring to the equestrian world a program that will create a perfect partnership with a horse and express how to deal with their different moods and personalities to achieve enthusiastic performances.

I have created a school to educate equestrians on how to handle horses at the foundational levels of horsemanship through learning the culture of horses. Horses need to be trained at the beginning stages of connection and their behavior needs to be shaped. The best way to do this is in a social manner without tack or fences so that the horse can feel a sense of connection in the moment.

My logo signifies to me that horses have different characters, moods and attitudes toward us created by our influence. We need to take all of this into account. The three heads show different moods as well as character types. The character types are lead, dominant and submissive. The moods are enthusiastic, willing and unwilling. The mood of the horse can be created from our influence or because of a horse's history or character. Whatever the case, we need to focus on developing a working partnership and shape a horse's character to fit in harmony with us not through force but through building friendship, respect and a language created from these considerations.

Carolyn Resnick METHOD
The Foundation for all Equestrian Pursuits

My Method is about shaping the character of the horse to fit in harmony with us by taking into account his moods and being able to put the horse in a willing mood so our leadership is followed naturally. It is our job to shape the character and attitude of the horse through the practice of rituals that are natural to horses. Doing this develops a horse to accept our leadership without question. By fashioning our leadership in this way, we win the respect and loyalty of a horse. By developing the willingness of a horse we also bring him well-being through the training process. We can also develop the horse to perform enthusiastically from the joy and responsibility we give to him.

You will develop team working skills both in yourself and the horse by using the same rituals and laws that horses use to create a cohesive herd. These are the same rituals that build deep friendships, respect and team working skills that create a united herd. I have named these rituals the *Waterhole Rituals™*.

Using the *Waterhole Rituals™* will bring people the ability to shape character and performance in a fun way for the horse. Adjusting your leadership and a horse's character at the same time, you will develop instincts and a strong ability to communicate with horses. Leadership that works through a connection in friendship, both for the horse and the human, creates a strong spiritual bond that you can rely on. By following the rules of the *Waterhole Rituals™*, the training of the horse is achieved through companion interactions that bring about a magnetic connection in performance like dancing partners sharing in companion energy.

I want to get people to really look at a horse as an individual and understand that the first thing to develop in a horse is a strong connection, respect, a willingness to follow your lead, an ability to communicate and a desire to perform. Training and performance without these qualities offers little reward to the horse and leaves him with no self-pride. The horse therefore becomes just a servant and will never perform to the best of this ability in the same way as a strongly bonded horse will. If one is looking for the full co-operation of a horse and a top performance, it is not going to come from impersonal training methods.

What's the Best Method to Train a Horse?

I often get asked, "What is the best method for training a horse?" However, I am not that prescriptive. So, for people who are really confused about all the different rules and methods of training a horse, I want to help you make your choices in deciding which way to turn.

Many times, it appears that all the rules are in disagreement with one another. How can this be? How does one sift through them and choose the right method when you lack experience with horses? How does one handle all these controversial expert opinions?

I can make it very simple for you - all of the methods work or they would not be methods, and all are based on rules that pertain to their program. The rules of the method guide you to the best results of that particular method. The best method is the one that is the easiest for you to apply and the one that resonates with you and your horse. So, pick one you like. If that works for you, then stick with it.

This is very important because practicing will cause the method to work and if it fails, then change to a new program. Most of the time people do not stay with the method of choice long enough. When the method fails, don't drop it, get help. In time, you will be able to use all methods well, once you develop your horsemanship skills. What will happen is you will begin to use methods and apply them in a manner that works for you.

Here are some guidelines and suggestions:

- Follow horsemanship rules to play it safe and to get you started
- Choose the rules that work for you
- Use the rules of horsemanship when they resonate with the horse, and when they bring about harmony and unity without the use of force and rules
- Don't force a horse because he needs to follow the rules; it could be your lack of skill
- Seek guidance that matches your needs and philosophy
- Break the rules when you know the way. Once you figure out what the rules are trying to accomplish and you have developed some skill, then do it your way if you like. This way you can change the rules to work better for you and your relationship with your horse
- If you are conscientious and if you are interested in the art of connection, then horses will have no fault insurance

Fast is Not Better: Is there Only One Right Way to Train a Horse?

We need to change the concept that there is only one right way to approach a horse and that the "right way" has already been discovered, and that the horse and human must cater to it, and that the best method is the fastest method. Fast is not better. Relationship is about time spent in connection. We need to recognize that better horsemanship is achieved through being continually educated by the horse; by adjusting our leadership to create a true working bond.

By training a horse in the moments he wants to be trained and by taking the time it takes to rebuild his enthusiasm when he stops liking it, we will continue to advance our horsemanship skills and hone our methods and in the process gain a higher consciousness.

From the horse we can increase our instincts and develop more respect for all life on earth, and discover a better way to be, lead, love and partner so that more meaning and fulfillment can be brought into our lives.

For horsemanship to be on the cutting edge, it should be a direct experience with the horse; a shared experience; an organic experience and a personal experience, for each and every horseman to be able to expand to new heights of awareness. Our world of horsemanship has been stuck over the years thinking that there is no room for change and better approaches. People get caught up with which is the right method rather than increasing their horsemanship skills and following their instincts and being considerate to a horse using common sense and treating a horse the way we would want to be treated. It is important to become aware that the horse is raising our consciousness from his presence alone. We need to see that horses can bring peace and connection to the world from what we learn from them.

My personal message is to bring awareness. If we are going to own a horse it should be our intention to care for him to the end of his life. That riding and training and the 24 hour experience the horse receives from being in captivity should enhance the horses' quality of life and self esteem. From a vigilant need to care for horses in this manner, horse training methods and horsemanship skills will continue to grow, expand and deepen.

My greatest connection and training that I share with horses has come from my ability to learn something new from my horses every day and seeing myself as a student of the art of horsemanship and never the expert. I have learned how to get my horses to cover for me from my lack of skill. When it happens, I feel blessed.

Training Can be Such a Pleasure

This morning I started thinking about what causes people to abuse horses when the horse doesn't perform for them exactly like they would like, or what causes somebody to overlook the responsibility of continuing to train their horse.

I came to the conclusion that people really do not enjoy the process of training. They don't realize that training itself can be such a pleasure.

Training is like opening up a package; we are really excited about just finding out what's inside. That ensures training is not abusive, because we really don't expect any bottom line; we are just happy with whatever results we get.

We look at the results that we have and then we continue on until we get the results that we want. Whatever happens is perfectly fine. It doesn't matter whether it happens in one short training session or over several months or even if we don't get it done at all. A person that really loves training and loves horses does not slip into being too submissive or too aggressive.

So think about how you could find the excitement of owning the horse not in the use of the horse but in the actual training. Because for me, the training is what causes life to be real pleasure because I'm never quite sure exactly what my day with my horse is going to look like. It stays fresh and alive, and I am happy that no matter what stage we are at in the training process, I can go out and train my horse and he happily volunteers to have that experience with me. That is exciting.

Training is Like Baking a Cake

Training can be analogized to baking a cake. You just take what happens, add in some interactions, allow the process to happen and all of a sudden you wind up with this beautiful dance, which is like the cake that you bake.

If you think about it, we do not have to change anything. It is just the process of putting everything together which creates the dance that we are looking for, which means we do not have to change the horse's nature. When you bake a cake, you do not tell the sugar to be anything. You do not tell the flour it has to be different. You do not tell the butter that it needs to be different. It is all about how you put the ingredients together that brings you your result. So, let us bake some cakes when we are training horses.

Sense of Freedom for Horses

I had an unusual life growing up in the desert with horses. Our horses were able to run free most of the day in a herd and go where they wished. They were loose and there were no fences to keep them from doing exactly what they wanted. The freedom, connection and performance I shared with them caused me never to really accept the conditions horses are faced with today. Horses are not free anymore and we keep them in captivity. This is one of the reasons I invented the *Waterhole Rituals™*. We have taken their land, called it our home and horses haven't any claim to the motherland that frees their spirit, leaves them to raise their families and keeps them together as they wish.

No matter how much some of us love horses, horses need more than love. If we cannot give them back their freedom, we can give them a sense of freedom by giving them companionship, the outdoors, shade, horse friends, grass to graze on, or rides and treks with them in the hills that call them. They need shelter, plenty to eat and drink, vet care, hoof care and a job to do that gives them a sense of accomplishment and self worth to replace the call of the herd.

We can return to them the rituals that they long for, so that they can problem solve, make decisions and believe again that their instincts serve them well. They should be allowed to snort into the wind with pride and to spend time in bonding and companionship doing absolutely nothing. They need to feel in harmony with us and to feel a sense of family and belonging. And even when we have done all of this and have given a horse more than a life of standing alone all day waiting for their master to break their boredom and their enslavement, they are still in bondage.

Our equestrian pursuits should not be about our pleasure or the sport, game or competition but about enriching the life of the horses. Something that feeds their spirit like their ancestors experienced when then ran free in their wild days of good fortune. When I work with the *Waterhole Rituals™* my horses experience a companionship connection with me at liberty. I feel the essence of the horse's spirit come alive sharing a magnetic bond in a herd of two in unity that is life enhancing to us both.

The Big Yes – Developing Championship Performance

This is a picture of my horse Stoney, who I had since he was two months old. He is performing *Levade*, one of the Spanish Riding School movements that is trained with tack. I trained Stoney to perform *Levade* without tack, at liberty in a full-size arena. I was able to do this because of the bond of the friendship I shared with him. By working with Stoney at liberty, I did not make the mistake of teaching him when he did not want to listen. Because he was free to choose, Stoney was able to lead me to a true understanding of horses, horse training, communication and leadership. He taught me to look for the big "yes" that is inherent in all horses.

When this picture was taken, Stoney had been retired from Spanish Riding School movements for several years. A photographer needed a picture of a horse at liberty performing *Levade* for a calendar. I was out of town at the time and could not help. With only verbal information about how to cue my horse, complete strangers were able to ask for and receive a perfect *Levade* from Stoney. In the photo, he looks like it was his idea to perform - and it was. His precision is awesome - a perfectly suspended rear on his haunches, ears forward, enthusiastic. In an open 40 acre field with a camera at his side, still Stoney showed his stuff! Looking past his elegance, what grabbed me is his joy to perform after twenty years of service.

He put in a champion performance. The kind that can only be achieved when it is the horse's idea to perform. This perfection must be managed from the highest understanding of horsemanship. In every champion there is an unbridled spirit. This spirit is the voice of my blog and what Stoney has taught me is what I will share with you.

EDUCATIONAL PROGRAM

Dance with Horses

I'd like to tell you some more about the amazing journey we have been travelling in my Fall and Winter Program. The curriculum is designed to prepare the mind to step aside and let go of the need to make sense of anything, and to return to the child mind and become truly present.

In general, humans have lost their ability to be present in the moment whereas horses are naturally present and because of this gap, a working bond cannot spring forth. Taking the time to become truly present in the moment is one of the many ways horses can elevate the human spirit. Once this present-ness is obtained, natural skills of connection with horses spring forth and the *Waterhole Rituals™* seem natural and easily understood. When this happens I then provide the class with all the Rituals and how to use them to develop a working bond.

The child mind learns quickly and with the curriculum, returning to this state is easily accessible. We need to step away from needing to know. Needing to know the formula and having to make sense of things means the mind not only loses the ability to grow to new heights but holds on to old patterns in general.

The *Waterhole Rituals™* are about letting go of what you know and getting comfortable with experiencing a horse with no agenda. In this way you build your understanding of a true heart connection with eyes wide open and discover a world of expansion.

As you grow from the natural process you develop a dancing leadership of give and take where boundaries are flexible and provide a way to bring out the desire in the horse to follow your lead rather than his own. You learn when to give in and when to set rules to win a horse's respect and friendship.

Each session has a theme and sometimes, a participant leads the class. Anne Birkhoff led a class on creative writing on a special horse that touched our hearts. Her ability to get everyone to write amazing details was gained by carrying the class to a moment in time that brought awareness to us as if we stepped out of a time machine. To recall the essence from our memories, Anne had us bring pictures of our favorite horse to class. Virginia brought something she had written that had great meaning, as well as pictures of her beloved horse that had recently passed away and a braid from her tail. It was truly a sample of creative writing from the heart. She laid out the pictures on the table with so much reverence, I was touched beyond words and her horse came to be so alive in my heart I could almost see her grazing on the lawn next to us as I listened to the story she wrote. (You can read Virginia's Story on p171).

My clinic is not about horse training, although training happens just as it did in the movie `The Black Stallion' when the boy and the horse were together on the beach. It is a spiritual happening in connection with horses, life and each other.

During the time we spend together, we have tissues on hand for our tears and laughter. As the facilitator, my job is to keep everyone in the present moment by offering the environment and the *Waterhole Rituals™* in a way that enhances the connection we share with horses.

Develop Better Body Language Skills and Lead Horses

I had the pleasure of sharing one of my 'Dance with Horses' clinic with Joy, a lovely lady from Denmark. I do so enjoy teaching and sharing my message and it's so nice to see so many people from all over the world finding resonance with my Method.

With this in mind, I hope to be working more closely in the coming months with my good friends: documentary film-maker, Stormy May (www.stormymay.com) and author and artist, Liz Mitten Ryan (www.lizmittenryan.com), to spread the word of a more natural approach to horsemanship and an appreciation of what we can learn from horses.

The 'Dance with Horses' course is a journey of self-discovery facilitated personally by me. It will be a re-awakening experience for you by helping you bring awareness to your personal journey through the art of mindfulness. Sharing mindfulness with horses in the moment brings us back to our authentic self.

I guide you using many of the *Waterhole Rituals™* as a way to help you win a horse's affection, develop better body language skills and the kind of leadership that draws horses and humans to you like bees to honey.

To acquire this ability we must communicate authentically with a horse. Nearly everyone has lost the art of authenticity because of the way our culture develops our focus and behaviors.

So how do we get in touch with our authentic self? That's easy. All we need to do is feel connection in the moment, stay aware of our surroundings, share with each other and be inspired to dance.

Each session follows a format of meditation, group sharing and guided wisdom from the book *Way of the Horse* by Linda Kohanov. During the course you will experience foot baths, shared stories, short trips in nature and dancing with horses to music because it is so much fun!

Lessons of the day may also be given by someone in the group if they feel moved to talk about a particular subject. The sessions are held twice a week for three hours and a complete course lasts for eight sessions in total. However because of the very personal nature of the course, I only take a few people at a time. Places will be very limited so I would advise you book early.

I am creating a space for people to make a true heart connection with horses and with each other, as there are a huge number of us that find a deeper meaning to life though horses and through sharing our experiences with others.

There is a way of being for both horses and humans alike that helps you achieve your dreams. Communicating with a horse in moments of mindfulness and without agenda is truly magical and life enhancing.

In this state of being we bring ourselves and the horses to a better quality of life. In this state of being connection with horses is natural. So let's come together and retrieve this part of our true nature through our love of horses.

Naked Liberty Audio Book Recording

I am very excited because this week sees the launch of the audio recording of my book *Naked Liberty*. I am honored too that my dear friend Liz Mitten Ryan, author of *One With The Herd*, agreed to read it.

The way I met Liz is a most amazing story. Computer life is pretty interesting and full of adventure. One night I decided to look for a horse painting, with the idea that my search might lead me to something I would like to own. I really enjoy art, so as I was shopping the Internet, I found an artist I really liked. I went through all her paintings and found the one that I would like to purchase and so decided to get in touch with the artist.

It turned out to be Liz. I had no idea that she was an author, horse breeder and communicator and she did not know about me either. I told her that I would like to buy her painting in the future. She asked me about my interest in horses and that is how we learned that we are both authors and horse communicators. I told her I would send her my book and she said she would send me a copy of hers. This is where it gets interesting because when we exchanged addresses, we found that we both shared the same street address – Summit Drive! So now, we refer to ourselves as the "Summit Sisters."

After reading my book, she called me and said that she enjoyed it very much. She also admired and shared in the message I am bringing to the world of horse and human connections. She then went on to say that she would bring the painting to me in person so we could meet and she could learn about my Method.

Since our fortuitous meeting, Liz has traveled with me and attended one of my clinics in Malibu, CA at Stephanie Abronson's ranch. She then got me on a radio show called Animals Talk Naturally that was interviewing her on *One with the Herd*. However, the original angle of the interview changed because it focused on our similar connection to the spirit of horses that included both our books. During the interview, I learned that Liz is a great storyteller and I loved her voice. It was then that I asked Liz if she would be the narrator for the audio version of *Naked Liberty*. She said she would and she has!

FUTURE VISION

The Sorraia Centre for Equine Facilitated Learning

For years I have had a vision of creating a permanent school for the general public where they can learn to study horses and embark on a voyage of self-discovery. Many people I have shared my vision with are excited about the school and its purpose. Like the *Waterhole Rituals™*, which are an evolutionary experience in learning, I envision the school will grow and develop in a similar manner.

The first five years the Companionship School with Horses will focus on the first two *Waterhole Rituals™* only so people get a true foundation in the understanding of horses. The school is meant to work in concert with the knowledge gained in the first five years and the natural evolution of the students, and my direction of the Method in the same way the *Waterhole Rituals™* are used to develop a relationship with a horse.

After the first five years, I would like there to be two schools in horse human relationships developed. The First School would focus on learning the nature of horses. The lessons would be learned through observations of herds in nature and through being in companionship in nature with them like I experienced as a child. There will be no training of horses only sharing space and watching carefully for the progress of the relationship to happen naturally and to become so bonded that riding is achieved without training.

The Second School would be to utilize all my Methods from Liberty Training, the *Waterhole Rituals™*, single lining, bridleless riding, drill team coaching and dressage training for horses and for riders.

Once both schools are in operation, all people attending the horse training school must simultaneously attend the Companionship School in nature, although those attending the Companionship School do not need to attend the training school.

Ultimately, all horses in the training school will come from the Companionship School that could be ridden without training and that exhibit a desire to learn and perform.

The School would be open to and cater to the general public. The purpose being to educate the public in how important it is to study the herd behavior of horses and how the pecking order is a successful effort in creating deep friendship and loyalty as well as a way horses achieve great networking skills, leadership skills, and social manners for survival.

The School will have a large horse book library, restaurant, picnic areas, a small theatre with a shop in the lobby, a large store and an art gallery throughout. There will be a bed and breakfast experience with horses consisting of seven yurts that sleep up to four people, a wedding ceremony site and a convention centre. It will also serve as a nice stop for people who are traveling by. Visitors will be able to keep up with the progress of the school through field tours and educational films made each month and that will be shown at the theatre every 15 minutes. There will be two films daily, one 3-D film that explains the pecking order, the rituals, and the purpose of the school and the other a monthly progress report of school activities in high definition film.

I would be at the Centre in charge of the guest experience, program development, quality control, instructors, the bed a breakfast experience and creating educational material from all the activities and points of interests that occur at the Centre.

Building Community Teamwork – Part One

Earlier I introduced the idea of a school or educational centre called the "Sorraia Centre". For those of you that are interested in the school and the ideas I have for it, I have written about it here and will continue to develop the direction of its studies and post these ideas on the blog occasionally for you to follow and support.

My vision for the Sorraia Centre beyond the cultural studies of horses is to highlight how students and teachers can work together as a team in reaching the goals of the school's programs. In our culture today, we have lost team working skills and the deep fulfilment and personal well-being that comes from serving the community, which I want to bring back to humanity.

To function well in a community project we need to enjoy the process of working and networking together along with strong, attentive and supportive leadership. It is important for both students and teachers to have a sense of pride in mastering team-building skills. I want to bring the public more awareness in seeing the importance of community to bring a sense of belonging and purpose to one's life. The most successful and rewarding community programs come from leaders who work hand in hand with the community and where the individual is allowed to participate in leading, with appropriate support of the program leaders.

My hope for the school is to demonstrate accelerated results by not being in a hurry, by enjoying the process and by developing better team working skills. I want the community to know and support an individual's needs as well the individual supporting the community projects. The goals we set ourselves will be reached with ease if we focus on creating a better connection through harmony and unity with one another. Team working is more effective through the enjoyment of the journey and the friendships that form.

Wild horses created a deep need within me to help humans seek out the harmony that is in nature and to discover the natural laws that support the individual in becoming stronger. Through my life's work with horses, I can bring attention to the fact that the pecking order of horses has the qualities to achieve a unified herd. This harmony supports the weakest individual due to the wild horse's sense of duty to the herd community. They have a phenomenal ability to work together as a team through balancing their needs between community rights and individual rights, something that does not come easily to humankind. I knew it was to be my life's work to bring a clear understanding to humanity of the social order of wild horses and how we can greatly improve our own communication system and support of our leaders by what we can learn from them.

Building Community Teamwork – Part Two

The program's study will centre around three wild horse herds consisting of caretaking lead stallions and their mares and foals on enough land to support 30 horses with extra feed when necessary. There will also be birth control management and horses relocated to proper environments as the numbers increase. The Sorraia Centre will be a model to show more effective ways for educating students and better methods in leadership communication through programs that bring more experiential learning, relationship and community participation.

To understand the culture of horses, the School will offer programs in horse behavior studies. How horses create their language and educate their young to bring about a unified herd in harmony, and how they achieve their ability to work together as a team for community survival exemplifies the purpose of the program. There will be an intimate study of the pecking order proving that it is a system that supports the community and the weakest individual rather than a system of survival of the fittest. There will be studies showing the difference in dominant horses and leaders and how both personalities work together to create unity and safety for the herd's survival. The study will show how dominant horses create the order and lead horses lead. The knowledge gained from the study of horse behavior and understanding how to use the *Waterhole Rituals™* to communicate with horses will lead to programs in human communication.

The School will bring this awareness to the public by creating tours, an interesting family stop, picnic grounds for casual observing of horse behavior, a restaurant, gift store, theatre and bed and breakfast experience. The theatre will show short 3D films about the *Waterhole Rituals™* along with a new film each month that will show what has been learned in each month of observing herd behavior at the School. There will be daily guided tours for the public by the student leaders to increase appreciation of horses and their culture. Visitors will learn how the environment and weather plays an integral part in the horses' well-being and will be a model of how nature works to support life on earth. There is also a school that will teach how to lead and interact with horses in partnership, and this will show that the horses enjoy training and performing with humans. The skill gained from this program will prepare future leaders in all fields of education, personal development and business.

The students will learn optimum responsibility, leadership, and communication skills. The program is being developed based on the depth of experience I have acquired over many years teaching horses, and teaching humans horsemanship and performance. My expertise is training horses through a natural evolution at liberty, dressage, bridleless riding and herd behavior developing a working bond using every day rituals I have named the *Waterhole Rituals™*. From observing wild herd behavior and how horses educate their young, I discovered the unwritten herd laws that develop tremendous networking ability, cooperation, and community loyalty. I also found that these laws are effective in teaching leadership and community to people and have the same capacity to improve relationship and networking skills. The focus of the method is on the quality of the relationship shared with the student and the teaching rather than the outcome and goal of the project. Today, people are more goal-oriented than community minded. If all parties have the power to communicate how to reach an ideal outcome for that day and the process is equally as life-enhancing as the goal, the result will offer the highest return. By focusing on building connection and enthusiasm, you can build truly effective humane leaders as well as create loyalty and friendships that are lasting and act as a resource for future networking partnerships.

CHAPTER TWO
IMPORTANCE OF UNDERSTANDING HORSE PSYCHOLOGY

HORSE BEHAVIOR

The Horses' Code

I'd like to talk to you about the rules that horses have with each other. This is extremely important to grasp not just because for me, it is the foundation of what I do, but because it is the foundation for all horse interactions.

Horses in the wild follow an unwritten code. A would-be leader needs to follow the code of the herd to win their loyalty and apply the code to win the position of leadership.

The code looks something like this:

- If I pay attention and accept your authority and leadership, you have no right to pick on me
- If you ask me to do something that is for my own good, I am happy to follow your leadership
- If I do not pay attention, I will lose my rank
- If you are a tough guy, we can see who is dominant right now
- If I cannot find a leader to follow, it is my job to lead

All horses know and respond to these rules. Horses can sense when their behavior is inappropriate from lessons they learned growing up with their mothers and lessons they learned from older horses in the family unit. The most important rule in the horse's code is to pay attention. One way a horse can gain rank over another horse without a direct battle is to catch his opponent off guard.

My focus today for training horses is designed to be fun and entertaining for the horse. I believe there is a bond that exists naturally between horses and humans too. The root of this bond lies in a universal language that is shared by all living things, a universal language that creates the natural teamwork I mentioned above. My methods of training rely on this bond, a bond of friendship first. This has been the cornerstone of all my work with horses and forms the foundation of my *Liberty Training Method*.

Major Behavior Types in Horses

In their everyday need for survival, horses have created a communication system that is noteworthy. Wild horses are like a society of nomadic people who have leaders of leaders. Because nature's habitat for horses is open rangeland, each horse has freedom to pick and choose a band of horses where he or she fits in and where his or her personality type is needed.

I have observed three major behaviors in horses: Leadership behavior, dominant behavior and submissive behavior. These behaviors are also the personality types as well. Herds are made up of the right balance of personalities, with each personality fitting perfectly in the chain of command. If the herd makeup is not harmonious, then this is when horses tend to move on.

An important difference between lead horses and dominant horses is that dominant horses show no interest in leadership issues such as where the herd should go for food or how to escape from danger. Rather, they are interested in dominance issues such as maintaining or raising their position in the pecking order.

For this reason, a lead horse is generally the most intelligent horse in the herd. In general, the higher a horse's rank, the more intelligent he or she is.

Over the years, I have seen that with horses put together in a herd by humans, the lead horse at first acts much like a horse with a submissive personality. The lead horse, whether it is a lead stallion or a lead mare, is simply waiting for the horses to sort out their pecking order. Once the order is established, he or she knows that the horses will naturally be able to accept his or her direction. Lead horses at first will avoid any conflict. I have even seen them run to escape from a dominant horse.

Fights are usually between consenting scrappers, while the submissive are protected by onlookers. From the herd instinct of horses, core values and laws are developed that support the needs of the whole community, from the strongest to the weakest individual.

Horses do not live gentle lives even though the natural condition they share together is spent in harmonious herd behavior. Harmony is achieved through leadership that doesn't come easily. Lead horses are responsible for keeping the harmony by enforcing fair social behavior with the horses that are too aggressive. They avoid physical conflict by enforcing rules of behavior through aggressive body language at the moment a horse would naturally run in terror.

This behavior causes a dominant horse to surrender to the laws of the community rather than his own unfit, dominant behavior. Lead horses learn early that dominant horses pick fights while lead horses ambush dominant horses that don't pay attention to the lead horse. There seems to be an unwritten rule that horses must submit to any horse that catches them off guard. In my training, this knowledge works like magic to teach aggressive horses to respect my authority.

Are Wild Horses and Domestic Horses all the Same?

I've often been asked whether wild and domestic horses are the same or different from one another. Here's my take on it.

Gifted animal communicators who work with wild animals are focused on making the same connection and follow the same rules of communication that my *Waterhole Rituals™* are focused on. Your connection and leadership with the *Waterhole Rituals™* are on the animals' terms and not on your own because of the mood and the ability to control the relationship. One minute you can have a connection and the next you do not. In fact it is easier to read a wild animals' shift in attitude than with a domestic horse.

The more we work with these shifts and acknowledge them and only ask for performance when a horse is willing and in the mood, the more we can create the mood that brings about a true partnership. It is very easy to read a wild animal's response towards you. The way to handle a wild animal is very simple: If they are leaving you, leave them alone and if they are listening to you, then you can direct them. With wild animals, it is very important to gain respect regarding your personal space and never enter a wild animal's personal space uninvited.

Using the *Waterhole Rituals* ™ you adjust your approach to fit in with the interest of your horse and you build cooperation around food in a manner horses can understand. Your horse learns what is fair and what is not fair in social interactions with you, just like they do in a herd that has worked out a perfect ecosystem. This way you win respect.

If you have a naturally polite horse and you are polite too, you will have a great foundation for riding. The horse learns that he can work with you and you will work with him rather than him thinking he has no power and must do what he is told. Adjusting a willing attitude in a horse will become second nature if this is where you put your focus. Practicing the *Waterhole Rituals™*, you will acquire an ability to create an approach that will suit your horse's personality and remove his resistance at the same time. I remove resistance under saddle in an indirect manner through the rituals rather than through riding. When the connection is achieved with the rituals, it will remove the resistance under saddle.

As you build the connection with your horse through using the *Waterhole Rituals™*, you will see your horse in a new light. You will see more clarity in what would make the relationship and performance of your dreams.

Proven Fact: Horses Pick up Tricks and Moves by Watching!

I was reading an article the other day about some scientists that were figuring out whether horses learned through watching or not and I found it fascinating that they came up with the idea that horses do not learn by watching other horses. It's just so silly that they don't know that they do!

When I went to Verde Valley School, aged 14 years, I took my three year old Arab horse with me so I would have a horse to ride. I wanted to show her but there weren't any horse shows in that part of Arizona. However, there was a rodeo coming to town and I realized that I could compete at the rodeo on her doing barrel racing. My mare had never actually done anything like that and, in fact, she'd only been under saddle a short while. As I said, she was three years old, so I had maybe only ridden her about 30 times but I wanted to compete with her all the same.

What I did therefore was to ride her over to the arena at our school and just sit on her and let her watch the other horses running the barrels because she'd never seen anything like that before. I did this for about a week and then the next week we went down there and walked the pattern until she could walk the pattern of the barrels without guidance.

Then the following week we trotted, then we cantered and so on. This was probably only about six weeks before the rodeo but we ended up winning the event.

I think that the main reason for this was my approach and also the week that she had watched. From there, I took that information and I've used it in my training programs ever since. If I need to teach a horse to do anything, especially something like a Spanish walk, I get another horse to do a Spanish walk in front of him. Then I give a treat to both of them and if I wait long enough, the horse that was watching will start doing the Spanish walk on his own. That's the way I have taught every single one of my horses to do the Spanish walk, as well as rearing, lying down and any number of other tricks and moves.

So the moral of the story, for me at least, is to learn from my own experience and judgment.

Spectacular Equine Behavior Achieved Through Copying

The story that I am going to share with you today is about a horse that you may have seen on some of my videos by the name of Panadero. He is an Andalusian Stallion and he is absolutely just the most expressive horse you could ever wish to meet.

Every day that I went out to see him he would run up to me and we would play this game where we used to run along the fence of his paddock. He would run along with me and then I'd ask him to leave and he would take off and run across the field before I'd call him back again. I would give him leaves off the tree and then I would go along the fence as if I was going to leave and he would run with me in the hope that I would continue to play with him. I'd stop again and pat him and let him give me a kiss and I gave him some more leaves off the tree.

We did this everyday whilst he was with me and when Panadero had finished his training he back went to live with his owner. We also had another horse at that time that was second in charge and he had never interacted with me along the fence or played the game. But after Panadero had been gone for a while, I could tell that this horse had made up his mind that he needed to move himself up in the ranks and he started playing the game with me.

It was absolutely spectacular because this was the kind of horse that didn't want anything to do with people, but all of a sudden, for no reason at all, that horse would call for me when I came out of the house and his ears would perk up and he'd look just like Panadero. He'd run up to the fence, give me a kiss and then run off again with his tail up over his back and then he'd come back again and run along the fence with me.

It was just amazing that a horse I had hardly interacted with at all before then, suddenly started to behave like that. So I really wanted to share this story with you because it just teaches us how amazing horses are and how they understand their position within a community.

Horses Do Understand Reasoning

A client of mine called me for some advice on how to get her stallion to cross a bridge; a bridge that he was used to crossing. She housed the stallion in a barn at night and put him out in a field with his mares during the day. The mares came in with him at night and were put out first thing in the morning to make it easy to take him out to the field later.

For some reason though, suddenly he would not go any further when he got to this bridge he had to cross. They did not want to get into a fight with him on this issue and had tried many different training methods before they called me. I asked them, "What happened at the bridge that might have caused him not to want to cross it?" She told me, "One day when the stallion was in the middle of the bridge, a stork flew out from under it and scared him badly and ever since that time he has become more and more resistant to crossing it."

After I learned more about her stallion and how well he was trained, I asked her to describe the surroundings around the bridge so that I could figure out a plan that might solve his problem. This is the advice I suggested that worked like a charm.

I told her, "In the morning, take the stallion to the bridge and tie him to a tree close to it." The stallion I was told was always reliable in being tied and they could trust him in not pulling back. I had her tell him, "You stay here; I am going to look under the bridge to see if there is a stork". Then I told her to go under the bridge, make some noises as if she was looking for the stork and then go back to the stallion and tell him in a very firm voice, "There is no stork or anything else under this bridge!"

From communicating to him in this manner, he walked over the bridge with confidence. I also warned her that if he should later decide to stop at the bridge again, to just repeat the process.

Nature Helps in Bonding with Horses

Horses prefer being with horses in the wild. The carrot of freedom and self-direction and community of the herd is stronger than anything that people have to offer so to develop your bond of trust with your horse, rather than getting the horse to join you, why don't you focus on joining the horse so that you can understand their life and what it takes to redirect their focus. Let these conditions take over your focus and be with your horse on their terms. Take this opportunity to fall in love with nature, discover how to be in the moment and at peace with what is; become aware of the system in nature and the community of the herd. Become a wildlife lover and enjoy the experience. Take pictures and groom your horse when he is itchy. Bring food like alfalfa and wait for him to finish it. When he finishes it, follow him if you can. Go with him if he will let you. Pay attention to the distance he would like you to keep.

Why is it that horses must follow our lead for us to feel good about the connection we share with them? They might have the same feelings we do. They might be saying why is it that to have a bond with you, I must go where you go?

Enjoy the time that you have to fall in love with the relationship as it is. If you become one with your horse in their freedom you can better understand their point of view and then when their point of view does not hurt your feelings, you will be better equipped to make choices to empower your leadership.

How Mares, Geldings and Stallions Communicate

Today I would like to talk to you a little about mares, geldings and stallions and how they respond differently when communicating with us.

Mares can be moody. In these periods I find that if I take the time to connect with them slowly in the beginning before riding or training on the days they are moody, they will come around and forget their sensitivity and work with me as consistently as they would on any other day. If I cannot turn them around on the days they are moody, then I give them the time off they need. Mares can be very fussy about trust issues regarding strangers and even with other horses. In my experience, mares will try harder than stallions and geldings to please you and when they don't please you, they get nervous and defensive. I think mares are more focused on reading the intentions of people than geldings and stallions. Mares can have strong opinions on what is right and what is wrong in regards to human behavior. Mares get along with other mares better than they do with geldings. I have noticed all horses may prefer one sex or color of horses to another. Some horses will prefer women to men or men to women.

Geldings need more encouragement to pay attention. Gelding a horse to reduce stallion behavior makes them quieter and easier to manage but after being gelded a horse can lose a certain amount of zest. To put the energy back, some speeding up exercises in the "warm up" may be necessary. I start off by using the last *Waterhole Ritual™ Liberty Dancing* which I used to call *Go Trot and Come Up* to warm up the bond and connection with any horse that needs more enthusiasm, focus and drive.

Stallions as well as geldings need to have exercises on improving the gas pedal and brake but once you have a stallion trained to be forward he will generally stay that way where a gelding needs to be maintained. Once a gelding is energized, they are almost as quick to learn as mares. They are more consistent and are easier to manage than mares and stallions. In a few cases, geldings can have the same behavior as stallions. When a gelding retains stallion traits, it can be due to the horse being "proud cut" or "late cut." "Proud cut" means a horse that was not properly gelded leaving him able to still produce male hormones. A horse can carry a certain amount of hormones after gelding that then continues stallion behavior even when the operation is performed properly. In the case of "late cut", they have developed their masculine personalities and they may maintain their attitude.

Stallions can be difficult to handle, however in many cases, if they feel that you respect them they are much easier to handle. People can make mistakes in trying to win respect with attempts to prove their strength and by trying to lower the position of the stallion. The best approach to take is to not start any form of training until the bond and respect are established first. You would do this using the *Waterhole Rituals™*.

More on Stallions and Connection

Right, we were talking about stallions and that they can be difficult to handle, especially if they feel you don't respect them or you try to lower their position.

Instead of fighting with a stallion to gain control after the bond and respect have been established it is best to put them to a task that brings connection like the *Uberstreichen* exercises or ask for something you know would bring back his focus, which in turn will bring connection. Sometimes all that is necessary is to take him to the place he felt connected with you because territory has a great affect on the attitudes of horses. For instance if a stallion sees a horse that causes him to get out of control I will take him back to the exact spot or area I was riding or working with him where he was last calm and connected with me. I make a choice once I am in the area that creates control and I might choose whether to ask him to stand and gain relaxation or to circle in a relaxed manner. I must be flexible and work towards connection and not be emotional and/or forceful if it creates more disturbances in the stallion. Stallions are better left in the hands of people who are skilled in stallion management. Stallions learn fast but not as fast as mares.

You must be able to think ahead and keep an eye on what is taking place around you that could divert a stallion's focus, which can change his attitude in a flash. Oddly enough, stallions are easy to train once you have developed the skill in how to manage them. Many times stallions appear to be born trained - it is their attention to detail that gives them the ability to learn. They also like having a job to do. The focus in handling stallions should be on building the care-taking instincts. It is important for a stallion to judge that your interest with them lies in wanting to "win" his respect and trust because of your interest to bond rather than dominate.

The *Waterhole Rituals™* help to work on setting boundaries with a stallion and showing him that you respect his boundaries and then allowing him to dissolve your boundaries when he is polite. It is important that he develops the friendship with you on his terms when it fits in with your terms. Some stallions are so hormonal that they are happier in life being gelded. Many times racehorses run faster as geldings than they did as stallions.

Stallions do not shy at things as much as mares and geldings and if they do it is generally a way to dominate the rider or horses that they are trying to impress. Many times young stallions need to grow into their confidence or need to have boldness diminished a bit by teaching manners and developing coping skills by a person who understands how to do this without creating more trauma for the horse. From practicing the *Waterhole Rituals™* you will develop your skill automatically to handle stallions, mares, and geldings.

I have noticed that people are focused on understanding an individual's personality rather than being focused on understanding the nature of horses in general. A horse will share with you everyday "who" he is. He cannot hide who he is. If you know the nature of horses, it develops your ability to handle any horse's personality in any situation. You will know how to handle any spontaneous situations that might occur to keep the partnership and performance at its best.

CHAPTER THREE
CONNECTION IS THE FOUNDATION

FORMING A RELATIONSHIP WITH YOUR HORSE

Learning From Horses

My family instilled in me that dogs learn fast, horses can too, and most animals seem to learn faster than humans. It was this idea that caused me when I was a child to understand that I needed to develop my ability to learn from horses so I could be on par with them.

Both sides of my family were horse lovers. The big joke in my family is that they were bound and determined to raise me to have an interest in horses, as if they could have stopped me. It is hard to say if my parents' intentions were to support my interest or that they purposely shaped me to love them as I do today.

My mother was a wonderful dog trainer; her greatest dog was a dog-named Ibliese, a miniature French poodle with a nickname Chicken Harry because he liked chicken. Chicken Harry could do all of the tricks the dogs in the Lassie movies could do, as well as being able to give direction to a stranger in a car without my mother being in the car, if Chicken Harry had been there before. He could dive down in water over 10 feet to retrieve anything. If my mother asked him to wait by himself, he would wait for any length of time and never move. He was an intact male and would breed a female only if he had my mother's okay. Everything my mother taught Chicken Harry was formed from the friendship he felt for her. My mother, when asking her dog to perform, spoke in a soft loving voice and would only have to speak to him once and her dog would spring into action.

My dad was gifted with horses and was very careful to keep me safe around them. His guidance led me to the connection I share with horses today. He shared stories in what to do and what not to do. I remember my dad telling me a story in how he did something unthinkable when he was a child that got him in a lot of trouble. He said he was being lazy and a smart alec at the time and he tied the horses to his back suspenders, thinking he wouldn't have to pay attention to his job while leading the horses in from the field. That night the horses took off on the way back to the barn. That stupidly almost cost him his life. You can imagine that I heard that story a lot from my family, wanting me to be careful and to think before I tried doing anything innovative with a horse, especially if it had to do with ropes and tack. My dad always preferred I work with our horses without ropes and any form of tack because of his experience as a child. I communicated with my horses mostly at liberty and rode bare back in the beginning. Not using tack to train a horse developed my skills in the communication and training of horses for competition as a junior rider. The horses I competed on were horses that I trained myself.

Because my family gave me freedom and cultivated my innovative nature, I began communicating with horses like my mother did with her dogs. I saw that my mother did not base her dog training on rules, orders and signals but more on the relationship she shared with them. I followed her example by training horses from the companionship I shared with them like she did with her dogs.

My life as a show horse trainer was quite enjoyable and spiritually fulfilling for the horses and me. Because of the deep relationship I had formed with them, they were my best friends. To create a winning performance in a horse I needed to establish a deep bond of trust before we began training. The winning performance came from the relationship and working bond we had built together. This is the secret to true performance in unity.

Building Equestrian Connection

This article is for those people who enjoy increasing their connection, performance and horsemanship from the direct experiences they share with their horses. If you don't have a good relationship with your horse, all you need to do is change your viewpoint, step back and start at the beginning.

1. Do what you can do
2. Stay away from what you cannot do
3. Build on what you can do in each moment
4. If you hit resistance, change to a program that builds back the connection

The good news is this is the way you go about working with any horse, whether you have a good relationship or not. This is my rule of thumb and why my horses like me so much. I never take them for granted. They also know they can never pull the wool over my eyes either because I have taken the time to really look to see whether or not they respect my authority. I have chosen a program that I know will bring me positive results.

Each day I focus on building a stronger and stronger foundation for the working bond, which is based on all of the elements of connection established during the *Waterhole Rituals™*. Before I start any training program with my horse I spend time reconnecting with him, enjoying who my horse is today and in this time I figure out what part of our foundation is solid and what part needs to be redeveloped.

I look at whether I have my horse's full attention. If I don't, I play the game horses play over grazing rights in the wild. Games such as eat all you want as long as you keep your eye on me. Or I might do *Leading from Behind* or I will follow you. Or I might do, I will wait for you to connect with me.

The horses understand my intent from my focus. They know my interest is to win their favor along with building respect that would produce a horses' desire to accept my leadership and to see my leadership as enjoyable.

I gain this connection by keeping the horses socially responsible to the herd laws. If I must return to respect, attention or attitude, I return their behavior to being responsible and polite in an unconditional loving way. They see me in different roles: as a mother, father, sister, brother, best friend, student leader and dance partner. I pick the role that makes the best connection and that brings out a horse's interest to learn and perform.

I want my students to fill the social needs of the horse. To bring enrichment to his well-being by spending time with him each day before asking anything of him so both of you can get into the zone to really feel a deep heart-felt connection.

Developing a connection with a horse is a courtship process and a parenting process. Once you experience working with a horse with this kind of connection, you will not want to work a horse in any other way. From this kind of connection, I can read a horse's mind and know when the horse's performance would be perfect.

Focus on building a connection, moment by moment, just like you would do with any relationship, horse or human. Rather than working with static rules, you develop your ability to lead without effort.

Deepening the Connection – Part One

Without effort there is evolution in the air and with our combined efforts expect a faster advancement and shift in consciousness in the care, custody and control of horses. By taking action, we are bringing awareness to others in how to share a natural connection with horses so that more people can bring a better quality of life to them.

Love is not enough when it comes to fulfilling the needs of domestic equine. Stopping abuse is not either. We can improve the everyday quality of the life of our horses by fulfilling their emotional needs through the companionship we share with them. I want to bring awareness to the 24 hour quality of life most horses are experiencing in stalls and pens around the world. Many of these horses are miserable from not having freedom and social connections. Horses are social creatures. We must take time with our horses every day in companionship to fulfill their loss of not being in a natural harmonious herd in an environment of choice with free range feeding.

When we interact with horses in friendship, enjoy hanging out with them and participate in the bonding rituals horses enjoy, this is a good place to start. We must also make sure that a horse has other horses around to keep him company, adequate shelter, good footing, dust control, fly control, worming, vaccinations, daily stall and paddock cleaning. It is important to check on their emotional attitude and health to make sure that a horse looks bright and happy. The opposite would be that your horse shows signs of depression such as standing in a corner not interested in things around him or her and not moving or the opposite, uninterrupted pacing. Be sure you are maintaining the horse's weight and check every day that your horse is chewing and swallowing easily. Keep his feet trimmed and make sure the horse is receiving proper exercise. Rule of thumb at my ranch is if a horse shows signs of colic such as rolling, getting up, and lying down often, etc., I call the vet.

I feel good about the responses to my blog to create a shift to a higher consciousness. My reward for my efforts is knowing that more horses have well-being in the world and care for horses is getting attention and focus out in the horse community.

One big change that I am aware of has come from a few people who have admitted to wanting to stop their aggressive ways with horses but the biggest change I have seen is that many people say they are not going to be silent any longer about the companionship they share with their horse. They no longer feel like the crazy minority but rather they are feeling like superstars on the cutting edge of an inevitable shift in consciousness that is taking place right here and right now that horses are leading us to.

Not only can we offer more lifestyle to horses, but also we can bring awareness that training and communication with horses still needs more refinement as well as more time invested to prepare a horse in his training. Many people are still forcing horses in a way that doesn't serve them or the horse. Most of these people would really like to know how to interact with horses in a way that is life enhancing to the horse and through your stories on my blog I can provide them a path that will help.

I hope to bring more change in how we communicate with horses and each other as teachers, leaders and parents. The first lesson for teachers, leaders and parents is that no horse or human needs to be forced or coerced in order to get results. Leadership in its most appropriate form needs to be a co-creative process where leaders offer the program and the recipients shape the approach.

Deepening the Connection – Part Two

We must spend more time walking in the shoes of our horses to realize how we can bring a better quality of life to our equine friend. Through the process of finding a better quality of life for our horses can we find a higher consciousness and a better quality of life for ourselves.

I want people to love horses because of their spirit, depth of character and the magnetic connection we share with them rather than the service we expect from them. What stands in the way of a love connection is expecting a horse to do what he is told and thinking that we have a right to force him to perform for us whether he wants to or not.

It is all about taking more time to develop a connection that would create a desire in a horse to want to fulfill our goals. The real magic and dance we share with horses, what I like to call the *Centaur Connection,* is achieved from the enjoyment we share with a horse and that the horse also enjoys being with us. The enjoyment of the journey is what helps us to make the right decision to reach our goals in any activity we want to share with our horse.

In the part of the world I live in, I regularly see people more interested in reaching their dreams as a way to achieve self-fulfillment instead of receiving self-fulfillment from the journey, and milking the moment and each lovely step for all its worth. Approaching life in the moment in this way is when life gets rich.

For all the people who are on the cutting edge of social evolutionary change for horses, let's not be silent. Instead, speak of your personal journey and of the connection that you share with our intelligent and loving horses, and show others how to better provide for the horses they love.

Remember, don't get lost in the cruelty of man or in our self serving needs but rather make an effort to speak of this new connection we are sharing with horses right here and now. In speaking from the heart, people will listen and this will create a new consciousness and responsibility to all things on Earth for the path we share with horses.

The last thing I would like to share is what horses have taught me personally.

What I have witnessed from watching horses in nature is that horses have an ability to know where community herd rules need to be adhered to by the individual and when to bend the community laws to help the individual's needs. From this I learned how to be a leader by adjusting my leadership communication so I could develop the performance of the horse and at the same time deepen the bond.

Fluidity not Formulas is the Key to Connecting with Horses

I am not against formulas and lessons in the training of horses and people. I am only against them when they are the only way you go about communicating and training horses.

Following formulas blindly, without question and without adjustment, can cause a person to lose their natural leadership ability, which then causes the horse to focus on having to pay attention to the rules rather than focusing on the connection.

I think that it is best for a person to hang around horses and horse trainers to develop a rhythm and a way of being around horses when things are right. For years, as one of the many ways I have gained my knowledge of horse training, I watched horses being trained by other people. It's a lot of fun and I can't think of a faster way to learn how to train a horse and develop your skill in the training of horses than by watching horses in nature, and by watching trainers that horses like. The way to really develop your skills is to be in the real world of horses, and to gain knowledge through hanging around and supporting horses and trainers. Don't try to fix problems you are having with your horse. Be fine with your horse the way he is or get a horse that has no problems.

First, one must spend a lot of time with horses when things are right and then make a pact with yourself never to put yourself in the situation that will cause a problem. If you walk into a problem, stop what you are doing and get back to a true connection with your horse. Learn to lead being a student of your horse.

For a person to learn easily it is important to recall and analyze the child mind. In this way one will not see the flaws of formulas and why they do not work but rather see their benefit and use them appropriately, meaning, to use them in a way that the horse has a willingness to enjoy the training process. This is why I wrote my book *Naked Liberty* from a child's perspective so the reader could return to their native intelligence.

Children are nurtured from hanging around horses with their friends at the barn site, pastures or anywhere horses are. I spent all day at the barn site being with, watching and playing around horses as a child, whether I got to ride or not. This need for a horse's companionship has a strong effect in bringing about the best side of a horse and your natural ability for making a connection with a horse and solving problems and using formulas effectively. Children can while away the hours in pure bliss with horses. Horses know this and it causes them to want to relate with them positively. From this activity, children learn how to connect with a horse in friendship, gain respect, and trust naturally.

As we get older, we lose our interest to hang around horses in this manner. We skip being around horses as our focus and get to the part where the horse needs to fulfill our interest to ride them and serve us. We tend to skip the natural process in how to create a true connection with a horse. As adults, we feel we can find our connecting with horses in books and formulas. Following formulas, rules, and lessons is not good for us when it is our only resource for relating with our horse. It can create a static mind and horses that become resistant because formulas have inflexible rules that are applied to every situation in the same manner, which creates no ability to be flexible, loving, patient and creative.

A person tends to turn into a one trick pony, wearing one hat for all conditions in a robotic and unthinking manner driven only by what they want for the horse. They do not usually know how to handle unpredictable behavior or fill the nurturing needs of horses or how to keep a horse in line. This kind of behavior has no magnetic energy to invite the horse to feel a need to connect.

Rigid formulas serve an important purpose in the beginning to bring clarity to all the important elements in the training of horses, however, formulas have a tendency to take away a horses natural desire to connect with us as well as to take away our spontaneous genius, natural knowledge and common sense like a child that connects well with a horse.

Working with horses is not about formulas, it is about fluidity. To be fluid and know how to handle your horse to bring out his desire and willingness to dance - this is the art of horsemanship. People who have a natural connection with horses are the most fluid in how to win horses' respect and friendship. They are able to motivate the performance by inspiring the horse rather than keeping pressure on a horse until the horse gives in.

The true art of horsemanship is to develop dancing leadership. Adjusting the mood and connection and building desire and clear communication is all that is needed.

Art of Energetic Connection

I find that a very important connection I have with horses comes from the subtleties and energy that we share back and forth. For example, how I choose to connect each time I have been away from my horse. I might choose to be focused on him and greet him with my full attention because that is how he chooses to great me that day. Or maybe I meet him with my focus on the world around us rather than on him to display that I have my finger on the pulse of life. This way I can win his trust in the moment and enforce my important position as a valuable friend and leader. I consider all these things when I reconnect with my horse.

I make these decisions by how I feel, how my horse feels at the time and where his focus is. If my horse's focus is on eating and he does not acknowledge me, I will sit down and wait for him to come to me.

For those of you who do not have the time, you could move him off his hay and wait for him to come to you and take it slow by continuing to move him off his hay until he comes to you to put on the halter. It will shorten the warm up time you will need before riding him by developing the connection in this manner.

If the horse is focused on something else besides you but is not eating you could lead him from behind until he loses his focus and starts to feel connected to you. After that you can make it up to him by scratching him where he itches. This approach will also lessen the time of your warm up under saddle. The slower your approach, the more purposeful your approach, the more influence you will have with your horse wanting to follow your lead and do his job willingly under saddle.

When I was a kid, I would mimic the cowboys I respected. I would approach a horse that I did not know like they approached every horse, thinking it might cause a horse to trust and respect me like it did for them. Sure enough the horses would show respect to me just as they did to the men I admired. Why not try it. It's quite amazing. If you do not know how good equestrians approach a horse, make an effort to watch someone you admire that does not have to warm up a horse to have a deep connection when they start riding.

In my training business I always made a point of building the dance with my horse in every moment before I got on a horse, so the first few steps under saddle we take together would be in total unity. If it were not that way, I would turn my horse loose and work at liberty or single line to bring the connection to perfection.

It is not easy to write about subtleties, especially when they have to do with making shifts of perceptions in feeling and focus. The reason I bring this up is that right now I am working on a meditation DVD in nature with wild and domestic horses that I believe will be very valuable in improving relationships and increasing horsemanship skills. I have always felt the strongest tool I have is to empower students to slow down and become present to the moment. Spending time with your horse and liking who he is will help you in knowing how to approach your relationship and training of the horse more effectively.

This is when the magic happens for me. Getting lost in the moment and then discovering how to go about training my horse always leads me to the best way to approach my horse on that day and in turn, that will bring me the best results.

My secret in turning out show horses much faster than my competition was this slow approach in the first five minutes instead of just grabbing my horse like everyone else, or sending a groom to fetch my horse. The groom could untrain my horse by simply leading him with the wrong energy or poor horsemanship. I have always found that being focused on the quality of the horse's experience in training and riding, and creating a fulfilling experience for the horse, gave me a horse that had more heart and desire to perform in competition and dressage than horses that were trained by focusing on training alone.

One of the biggest problems horses have with humans is how they see where a person puts their focus. Most people, especially people who love their horses, are so focused on the horse that they lose all ability to know the conditions around them. I started noticing this with people drawing horses. Most often times the horses were drawn with extreme care and competency but as you look at the picture as a whole the only thing on the page is a horse floating on a blank piece of paper or the background was drawn with a lack of skill so it looked like two different people had drawn the picture.

I point this out because this can really disturb a horse if the only thing on your mind is your horse and what you are doing. A horse can feel a bit put off, thinking you are giving too much focus to him, which can give off a predator vibration. Think about it; a predator is not focused on his environment only on his target. I have actually caught feral cats that would never normally be caught by waiting for them to be focused on a mouse. I could walk right up to the cat and catch it.

Your energy can be read wrong by your horse even though you are sending him messages of love because the vibration resembling that of a predator is very similar. A horse is more focused on everything that is around him and if we can approach him in this manner, he feels more at ease. It is more horse-like. I focus on the horse and on the environment and the changing conditions in the environment all at the same time. If you are planning to lead your horse on a line, he wants a leader that has their mind on the pulse of life and a concern for the environment.

I hope this helps you understand how subtle the differences are between making a good connection with your horse from a bad one, and provides you with food for thought on the art of energetic connection.

Telepathy with your Horse

Today I want to add to the story about Panadero and his Spanish Walk. The last time I had worked with him his Spanish Walk had been very green and he could maybe only do about 25 feet. When I asked him for it three months later, he had mastered it like he was a seasoned horse.

So what I wanted to add was that one of the other reasons he did the Spanish Walk so beautifully was it was something that I could feel in him that day because of the relationship we had developed beforehand. I had asked him to do something else but he did not do it immediately. He was telling me that what he wanted to do something else instead and telepathically I guessed he wanted to do the Spanish Walk.

Sure enough, when I asked him to do it, he just jumped at the opportunity and did it for about 100 feet, which was something he had never done before in his life. A woman who saw this asked me how I had got him to do that. I said simply that he'd told me that he'd wanted to. She asked me how I knew that and this is what I told her.

If you focus on shaping a horse's behavior and developing the enthusiasm of the horse, you develop the skill of being telepathic because you are both working with the Method instead of forcing something on the horse. You apply the Method around the horse's behavior and when you do that and give it to him in doses he wants to receive, you develop this telepathic relationship with your horse.

If you think about it, isn't this how horses are in the wild or even in a paddock? When one horse in the herd senses danger, don't all the horses turn and run as one? The same goes for shoals of fish or flocks of birds in flight. Don't you think it would be useful for you to have that same ability with your horse?

Difference Between Respect and Dominance with your Horse

In this article you will find a question from Dee in California about the difference between respect and dominance with your horse. Dee writes:

To me, as a new horse owner, there is a fine line between gaining respect and being dominant. I really don't understand the difference. When I try to get my horse to stand still by the round pen railing so I can mount him bareback, he either steps backwards or swings his hindquarters away from the fence. Every time he moves away, I send him out for a few more rounds in each direction and then finally he remains still so I can mount him. I feel like I am scolding him for not doing what I asked him to do. I don't enjoy making him work so hard, but it seems like it is the only way to accomplish what I am trying to do. My horse is like a puppy. He is my new best friend and he is adorable. I have never been happier. Do I have to be dominant in order to gain respect?

My answer to that:

You are right, having your horse do laps in the round pen until he gives up is the wrong approach as a way to mount him, as it is a form of punishment. I bet he doesn't like you any better for it either.

The solution to getting your horse to stand still lies in good old fashioned training and a little change in approach as to how you go about mounting your horse from the fence. You may have heard the expression "one step at a time", well, what I am going to suggest to you is "one pause at a time".

The first step is to give your horse a big kiss and know that more training or maybe just a different approach is all that is necessary. Don't be in a hurry to mount you horse. Focus on developing his mood to stand still before mounting him by hanging out at the fence until he completely relaxes each time. This might be all it takes to have him stand still for you when you get on him.

If this approach doesn't work there are many wonderful methods you could use to teach your horse to stand while you mount him from a fence. I would advise you to look at all of them to widen your horsemanship skills. However, this particular program will do the trick for you and your horse.

Start by training your horse to not move off a spot you ask him to stand on, a spot that he would have a tendency to stand on naturally. If he fusses, just stand there till he is quiet. Once he is willing to stand on request, ask him to stand in many different areas of the round pen and spend some time grooming him. Then groom him by the fence as he already knows to stand still when he is being groomed and this will again get him used to the fence. Then teach your horse to stand still as long as he can in the center of the round pen while you walk around his body holding his rope loosely without contact. If he moves, place him back on the spot you wanted him to stand on.

Take whatever time it takes to teach your horse how to stand on different spots you have placed him on. Do one hour's worth of training with your horse. Then walk your horse up to a mounting block and say "whoa" and stand at his head and pause with him for a couple of minutes or more. Repeat by walking him around and then returning to the mounting block for another dose of standing still on a dropped rein. Continue this until your horse is trained to stand still in this manner. Then repeat the same exercise with you standing on the mounting block. Then teach him to step sideways to the fence you will be mounting him from and have him stand still for a minute or two, repeat this many times. Then sit on the fence and have a friend help you to move him to the spot you want him to be. Work with your horse from this position until you do not need your friend's help.

One of the things I always recommend people do if they want to develop a better (working) relationship with their horse is to just sit in his paddock to keep him company. This alone works wonders. Also do lots of grooming in his paddock at liberty. This will cause him to become more accustomed to standing when you are around.

The *Waterhole Rituals™* will develop your skill and understanding in what is fair to do to a horse and what is not. It will also develop a working bond with your horse, which would result in him naturally standing still for you. When a horse's behavior is not to my liking, I fix the problem with more training or more building more connection with the *Waterhole Rituals™*.

Before you train, be sure your horse is happy with his environment and is relaxed. He should enjoy your company, have a willing attitude and not feel fidgety. Any time your horse becomes fidgety, stop your training and focus on the connection and relaxation. When everything is working between you and your horse, you can return to the training program.

Bomb Proofing Horses... or Not

I have never spent much time bomb proofing horses because with the *Waterhole Rituals™* I provide a horse a feeling of safety in my charge and they follow my lead without question because of the relationship I have establish with them. Before you consider bomb proofing a horse, I would advise you to first, get the go and stop buttons working on your horse at liberty, as well as teaching a horse to be polite, respectful and willing to work with you creatively in any given moment. What your horse is lacking is an understanding in how to respond creatively and with interest.

It is a good idea while bomb proofing your horse to ask your horse to leave the area at a quick trot as well as to stand still, work between these two requests. Horses are capable of giving many different responses to the same thing if you train them through a combination of routines and creative spontaneous interactions. I can crack a whip very close and all around a horse's body with no response if I wish. The next minute I can ask him to leave very quickly just with a signal from a reed. From the training I give my horses, they can go back and forth between these responses at a moment's notice. I do not want my horses to be trained like robots, I want them to listen to me and not get lost in just performing things from a routine.

I create a true working bond where the horse is always focused on working with me as a partner, not trained like a circus bear or a horse that decides you must give him a treat for something you did not ask for. There is a way to think smart and develop a horse to be what you need him to be through creative planning. Here is an exercise you can do to "fix" a horse that is unresponsive due to bomb proofing or any other reason.

Have a friend stand outside the arena from your horse along the fence about 25 feet down with some hidden treats and ask your horse to leave with the signal you would like to use and then have your friend shake the treat bucket and stick it through the fence so the horse can have his reward. Repeat. This is a simple solution that a horse learns quickly. Be smart and plan this so it functions well for you by not tipping off your horse to the fact that a grain bucket is there.

Here's another idea. Have your friend stand in the area you hope to send your horse to with a hidden, small bucket of carrots or grain. Stand about eight feet away from your horse then with your intent and body language move forward quickly towards your horse using my reed and wave it all around his space and tell him to go. Send out big energy. You can point and point again repeatedly in the direction you want him to go. Keep this up until he walks away. He will walk away eventually because he will not stand there forever. Remember, it takes the time it takes. After you give the command to send your horse off, have your friend shake the bucket of carrot or grain and have your friend call the horse to them.

As soon as he walks away have your friend give him a carrot then have your friend repeat the same commands you did to move the horse back to you. Be ready to give your horse a carrot when he returns. Try to keep enough urgent energy in your body language to get him to trot back and forth between you. In between, you can work on asking your horse to stand still while you wave things around him and when he stands, he also gets a carrot. Your skill will let you take this exercise to the extremes I have described with my horses in that I can send it away fast or slow or have them stand still on one spot as long as I need him to stand.

Remember get the gas pedal and brake working on a horse before bomb proofing. It is a lot easier. Next, remember to get him to go between standing still and go trot and not to lose either response.

HOW TO BE A LEADER

Leadership with Horses is not about Self-Serving

My first lesson on leadership was when I was a little girl and was taught to me by a lizard.

In the olden days, the milk cartons had little tabs that you pulled up and made a little tiny hole in the corner of, so that when you turned it over, it would pour. It kind of made a natural spout and then you stuck the cork back into that little hole. They were little and cute. I liked them. I don't know why we've ended up with what we have today because I can never get them to open up, but anyway, back to my story.

So I figured out that if I left the little tab open and left the carton outside, I could possibly catch something in it. Well, on the third day, I did! I went and looked in my milk carton and found I had trapped a lizard. I closed that tab really fast and was so excited. I carried that little milk carton around with me and showed it to my mother and said, "I have caught myself a lizard!"

She looked inside and she asked "How long are you planning on keeping that lizard in the milk carton?"

"Well! I was thinking maybe it's mine now. It's my pet and I'm going to keep it forever."

"I don't think the lizard is going to like being in that milk carton." she said.

Well, at the moment, I wasn't really keen on that idea and so I carried that lizard around with me all day. At the end of the day though I had to turn him lose and that was one of the hardest things I ever did. But it also helped me learn about self serving acts.

All day I figured that the lizard was going to be totally happy in the milk carton because I wanted him. But that wasn't really the case, you see. So, when we are looking at leadership, let's really evaluate how it is we are using our leadership if we are really being honest with ourselves.

So when you are using the *Waterhole Rituals™*, you are not looking to gain anything; that's not what leadership is about. The rituals are only concerned with developing the relationship, the right sort of relationship between you and your horse and not one that is self-serving to you as the leader.

Equitable Partnerships through Leadership

If you lead your horse in the moment and he feels a companionship connection, it inspires him to follow your lead like music inspires a dancer to dance.

I have focused my life on figuring out how to get a horse to accept my friendship and for it to be as strong as the friendship he shares with other horses. From studying herd behavior, I have gained this connection by getting a horse to accept me as a family member and trusted companion. Not that he is a part of my family but that I am a part of his. I develop a friendship and trust by communicating with a horse through the daily bonding rituals that I learned from wild horses.

From the bonds I developed with wild horses in nature, I discovered that communication with horses was rather easy.

The reason the bond with horses and humans is usually is not as strong as the bond that horses share is that there is a cultural and language gap amongst other obvious reasons. To bridge this gap, the horse must either be domesticated to our ways or we must follow a horse's protocol and cultural laws. If we want to create a lasting bond, harmony and order, the key is to follow the protocol and culture of horses. Their protocols are about creating well-being, responsibility, teamwork and unification between the herd and the leader working together. From this, a one-minded connection is achieved. We are drawn to horses like bees to honey and we know it has something to do with their spirit and heart that we would like to experience and have for ourselves.

To be fair and equitable partners, we must first encourage the horse to bond with us. A true connection can only be formed when the horse feels that they have drawn us to them. This requires us to wait for a horse to be attracted to us without any influence, other than our presence sitting in his territory. This then comes from a natural process that has not in any way been forced or formulated

What I have generally witnessed is that the horse and human bond is based on the horse knowing he hasn't any choice in the matter. He will then falsely bond with a human because he feels it is better to do so and there are no other horses around that he can connect with. This formula does not allow for any extemporaneous interplay between the two.

When a true bond occurs, it socializes horses to feel good about their relationship with all humans. In the process, your horse learns how to be polite and respectful and accept direction through an inviting process that brings more life experience to a horse.

Being a friend to a horse and taking no leadership position offers no security and is a bit boring to a horse once the initial bond is formed. It is our job to shape the dominant nature of a horse to be social and polite. We do not need to change his dominant nature we need to bond and offer leadership when he or she wants it. A lead horse that has been chosen allows the followers to control and shape their leadership behavior. When a lead horse is respectful, the follower feels honored and in control of the leadership which brings the follower to feel a loyalty, responsibility, and trust. Both parties shape the other as a way to get to know one another and to be able to create a true working partnership. Horses need to work out a social order to develop deep friendships and horses need freedom of choice in social interactions.

Adjusting Your Leadership to Keep Attention

If you can keep adjusting your leadership to be more dependable, flexible, understanding and intelligent, the horse is more willing to form a loyal partnership and put a greater effort into his performance. The biggest mistake people make in their relationship and communication with horses is to not understand that the development of leadership with horses should be spent in managing the connection, bond and trust through attentiveness. Being attentive, you can respond to the changing attitudes in the horse and the environment and keep a horse willing before he gets out of hand. If you do not have respect and trust in a horse, you are unlikely to be able to tell him what to do and in the same breath expect him to take care of you. This kind of horse is hard to find.

Because horses are prey animals, when you take away its ability to escape from a predator by controlling him under saddle or on the ground, you are put in the role of a leader that will protect him. Horses are very observant on how focused you are and take this as a sign of your leadership ability. The horse will judge your ability to lead by testing your authority and leadership by seeing if they can push you around here and there. If they can, then a horse feels you don't really have the leadership ability to keep them safe and that they are better off protecting themselves by resisting your leadership and following their own. Fixing this problem is not about proving your capabilities with an aggressive attitude or forceful leading but rather by providing attentive leadership and by choosing how you communicate.

You know me by now; I am more about horsemanship, relationships and how to connect with horses than training or fixing problems. I also feel that horses do not owe us anything. We only have a right to train them, ride them or use them for their companionship if we are attentive to their needs and the horse is willing.

If you work within the connection and have good horsemanship skills, you will find that horses enjoy being in service and enjoy our company without any need for fixing problems.

As I see it, the horse community in general lacks trust that the natural magnetism between the horse world and our world is strong enough to make force unnecessary. The way we treat our horses in general is the way we treat ourselves, our children, our partners and most everyone in our lives. So learning how to connect with a horse without force or the need of an aggressive attitude is a really good thing. Horses like strong leaders but there is a big difference between strong leaders and forceful leaders. What we are looking for is a balance between feminine and masculine needs and qualities in appropriate measures to have an enthusiastic working partnership.

Based on reader responses, here are the results of everything you would like your partner (man or woman) to be. Think about how this relates to your relationship with your horse.

Attribute	**Preference**	**Attribute**	**Preference**
Loving	16%	Sensitive	7%
Honest	16%	Supportive	6%
Kind	15%	Strong	6%
Fun	12%	Respectful	6%
Attentive	9%	Intelligent	6%

Creating Attentive Partnerships

Previously I was talking about horsemanship, trust and connection, which led me to ask the question about what you would like your partner to be like. Now the reason I asked this was, and this is going to sound a bit out of place, but a horse wants to be treated like a woman wants to be treated.

In general, what horses and women want is a true attentive partnership and courtship. Both women and horses want to be protected also. Woman can see they are like a horse and they respect the power in the horse's spirit that they know is within their own understanding and nature, and they want to take care of the horse in the way they would like to be taken care of. When attempts at leadership do not work, usually people are not following the list but rather treating a horse like a child and not a partner. We need to be a parent, partner, leader and friend in the right moment.

A woman in general would rather have the power of a horse than the power of a lion. Speaking in general, a man wants the power of the lion and the support of the horse, the same thing he would from a woman. When little girls are drawn to horses, they usually want to be a horse. Little boys who are drawn to horses are more likely to imagine that the horse can take them into battle and they ride a high spirited, almost out of control, broomstick. When I was growing up, I was the horse and I rode a well behaved broomstick that I loved as my imaginary horse. And

I rode horses, read horse stories and dressed in cowboy and cowgirl clothing and played on the floor with horse figurines with other horse crazy kids, as well as coloring in picture books of horses.

When we take a look at people who have a way with horses, you will find they exude a certain ability to take care of any situation and women are really drawn to this. But more than that, what they really want is to connect with a horse and gain the strength that a horse possesses for themselves. In general, women believe that their personal power is gained from developing a heartfelt bond with a horse and when this happens the horse will naturally allow her to ride from the bonded trust she has formed.

When children become the horse, what they want is that horsepower inside themselves. But being able to harness that ability and use it in the practical world takes practice and a combination of both masculine and feminine reasons in wanting a relationship with a horse.

The horse community in general lacks belief in the natural magnetism of horses and humans and so they end up using force. This first thing that is important in getting along with a horse is to be attentive without force by staying in charge of what your horse is doing. A big reason horses develop behavior problems that need fixing is that attentiveness to directing a horse was not maintained.

The lessons we can all learn from connecting with a horse without force or the need for aggression can be really beneficial. The way to develop this ability to lead without force is through attentiveness. If you want to learn attentiveness, know horses and gain a connection with your horse, then practicing the *Waterhole Rituals™* will get you there faster than any other way I know.

You need to practice using the rituals on easy horses at first and must have a natural ability with horses in general to use the rituals on your own. If you want to speed things up, then a private clinic with me can help you gain the rudimentary skills you will need to be able to work on your own with the *Waterhole Rituals™* and to gain the skill to become your own horse whisperer.

The Importance of a Flexible Leadership Style

Connection is a two way street. To truly get along with a horse in shared partnership we need to have social leadership skills. If we can keep adjusting our leadership style to be more flexible, understanding and intelligent, the horse is more willing to form a loyal partnership and put greater effort into his performance. It's all about being present in the moment and fully awake and knowing exactly what to ask a horse to do that starts the dance, backed up with the belief that your horse will perform and then letting the horse perform without holding him to it.

A good equestrian rule to follow is that resistance should almost never be met by force, when training a horse. When you lose the dance you must recreate the connection rather than using pressure. Slowing things down gets rid of the need for force. You can make a strong demand without force when the horse feels responsible and knows the rules. Horses love rules and boundaries and even enjoy having them enforced. The most important part about enforcing a rule to a horse is to use proper timing and attitude. You have to see things from the horse's perspective. But first you must be able to get the horse to feel responsible; so in correcting the horse they respond with an "oops, sorry!" attitude without feeling intimidated in a negative way. It is my intention to guide people to the skills required that are not available in books on the finer points of leadership and understanding the mind and nature of horses.

When I am with a horse he has my full attention. It relaxes a horse. I keep my focus on my horse constantly when he is in my charge at liberty and with tack. My constant focus gives clarity in how to lead my horse properly and it will help you with your horses as well.

Here's an example on how I manage to keep a connection with my horse. If a friend comes up and talks to me, I don't give them as much attention as I give my horse whilst I am speaking. If I am talking to someone, I expect my horse to stand quietly and to be focused on me from the attention I give to him. My focus is to keep him quiet while I am talking. If I cannot do that, I excuse myself and talk later.

Many times, I see people letting a horse pull on the rope in order to get to some grass to eat whilst they are talking and then turning around and hitting their horse for not paying attention. It is too much to ask a horse to stay focused if you are not focused. It would be better to take the horse to the grass and let him eat rather than allowing him to pull you there. This way you stay in charge of your horse. Look ahead to what decisions your horse might make and be strategic in how you gain his cooperation rather than reprimanding him.

A consistent connection from maintaining your focus and leadership will result in a horse constantly staying connected to you. This state of being helps a horse to trust his handler. Allowing a horse to pull on a rope will result in you having to use strong rein aids when riding. What happens on the ground will affect how the horse rides.

CHAPTER FOUR
TRAINING BY MY METHODS

WATERHOLE RITUALS™

Centaur Connection **– Horse and Horseman Connected as One**

Being in the horse industry and being a horse lover on my own personal journey, I have seen a lot of personal growth in people due to the impact that horses have played in their spiritual evolution. I have seen trainers grow and change from hardened individuals to philanthropists and students turn into masters. I have seen first-hand the physical healing effect horses have on humans. All of these people that I have known over the years have horses to thank for their spiritual growth.

I feel that the biggest influence a horse has on me comes in the moment that I feel a connection between us as one - the *Centaur Connection*. I have an overwhelming appreciation and gratitude for the friendship that arises in these moments, the *Centaur Connection* that comes from our training experiences together. This experience catapults me into an overwhelming awareness to all that surrounds me in nature and to the universe as a whole.

Using the first *Waterhole Ritual* ™without going on to the other rituals offers a lifetime of opportunity. Staying with the first *Waterhole Ritual™* offers us the opportunity to continually increase our knowledge and our ability to learn and experience the ultimate happiness to be shared with horses without ever needing to share the next rituals.

The purpose of the first *Waterhole Ritual™* is to help a person to open their hearts and to lose the need for agenda and a desire to change the horse. In this way, we can begin to understand how to use the *Waterhole Rituals™* in a loving and responsible way.

Using this natural experience you will develop a know how to properly apply the *Waterhole Rituals™*. As you become more knowledgeable, you will get closer and closer to the ways and mind of horses.

Trying to apply the *Waterhole Rituals™* without the natural involvement of the relationship and without a connection to your horse is not how I intended the application of the rituals to be used.

The most important aspect to the rituals is to allow the connection to continue to grow in the most effective and natural way. Believe it or not, it is not important to me whether you move on to the next six rituals or not.

As our awareness grows through the connection we share with horses, it will deepen our wisdom, joy and connection to all things that we seek and have. It is my hope that from staying present in the *Centaur Connection* we will become increasingly aware of the unity and joy that exists in every moment. As this awareness grows, it will bring us to have more appreciation and love towards all things. By allowing our newly found awareness to lead us, it will bring greater meaning and appreciation to our life and a desire to be in community with all things and to be nurtured by serving others.

Sharing a *Centaur Connection* with a horse seems to affect many of us in this way. So many in fact, that in my mind, the horses' assistance in the spiritual evolution of the human race cannot be denied.

Practice Makes Perfect with the *Waterhole Rituals*™

As you might have guessed, I'm a very practical person. I learn by doing. Ultimately though, we all must learn by doing as there is no alternative and this is especially true with horses. I do hope that you enjoy watching my DVDs and reading my book but I have to tell you that unless you get out there and put them into practice, you will never know what sort of results you might get.

I recently had a lovely email from a lady called Madelaine. Here's what she had to say:

Something extraordinary happened today that I need to share with you.

I just received your DVD and your book. I watched the DVD and started to read the book at home, whilst sharing space with my horse. (What an exciting life you have with horses).

I have been playing a lot with my mare in recent years. I am a clinic junkie and studied most of the big names seeking answers on how to improve communication with horses because I am tired of all the emotional abuse and neglect we often unconsciously give them because we don't take the time to understand them.

I thought I had a good relation with my mare (Bravada) and I still do believe I have but recently she snapped at me twice coming out of her box. Actually, I was caught completely off guard and was extremely surprised and shocked (kind of insulted). I went looking for answers and this is how I discovered your site and Method. So far, I received the best explanation ever: bond and trust do not mean respect. Horses play dominant games and snap from behind if we let them lead from behind. It is their nature.

On Wednesday, I played with Bravada Sharing Territory, Saying Hello, Leading from Behind, Magnetic Connection, Go Trot and Come Up and Taking Territory. In that order. Magnetic Connection did not work too well because she would leave me if I turned the opposite way. Go Trot and Come Up got her annoyed because I trained her to free lunge around me connected with a nice bend at the poll and pushing from behind. I do clicker training so I normally would click at her when she was doing well. I did not and saw that she was getting upset; she bucked and had a tense jaw. I quit. I reviewed your DVD and learned that we should not do Go trot and Come Up if the Magnetic Connection is not good.

Today, I did Sharing Territory. I felt she was really in tune with me so I tried the Magnetic Connection. Wow, we were trotting, stopping, and turning right and left shoulder to shoulder. She did get a few carrots along the way though.

After that I decided to ride a little, which was magical. I don't know if it is due to your Method or not since I am quite new to it, but it was the best ride ever with my horse. She gave me passage and piaffe movements that I had been practicing or trying to accomplish for more than a year now. She was a joy to ride, the transitions were smooth. I got the best canter strike off ever. I had the feeling of being on a cloud, it was light and effortless. I felt we were both so in tune and in harmony. I rode for 15 minutes only, maybe less; it was too good I had to acknowledge it by giving her the ultimate pressure release (dismounting), treats and hugs.

I have only been doing the Rituals for the last two days. Could that be it? How often do you do the Rituals? Once or on a regular basis? Some Rituals more than others depending on the state of the horse at that moment?

Here are my answers to Madelaine, which I think make a good summary of what we are trying to achieve:

I use the *Waterhole Rituals™* every day that I see my horse because it brings them a sense of community and freedom and well-being like they would get with a herd of horses that they were bonded to. They get joy out of it like a dog would playing catch or chasing a ball.

The *Waterhole Rituals™* prepares the heart, mind and spirit to focus on wanting to share and communicate like a dance partner. Each Ritual is to be used as a test to check out the heartstring of connection that it represents.

The first Ritual, *Sharing Territory,* is to get the vibration of the bond going.

The second, *Saying Hello,* is like re-doing your vows of respect by showing the horse that you will only lead in the moment he is willing to follow and never with force. This develops and establishes trust.

Taking Territory creates respect. However this Ritual should in most cases be used very sparingly. I find that in a lifetime of a horse I might have to use it four or five times. If you have a horse that is very disrespectful, use it as much as necessary to gain respect. If you cannot sneak up on the horse to take territory it should not be used. You would then use *Leading from Behind* to get the job done.

The *Eye Contact Ritual* puts in the mind of the horse that he needs to stay focused on you.

Leading from Behind develops a work ethic and makes fear and aggression evaporate. Leading from behind also builds courage in the performance itself as well as developing camaraderie.

Companion Walking in the Magnetic Connection will only work if the other strings of connection are truly in place. If your horse will not companion walk, don't "train" him to do it. Figure out where the failure of connection lies and rebuild it with the appropriate Ritual.

Go Trot and Come Up (now called *Liberty Dancing*) is to be used when *Companion Walking* is consistent.

Madelaine wasn't afraid to go out and try the rituals and although she maybe didn't get them straight off, she had a go, made progress and continued to practice.

I had a follow-up email soon after that said she was able to get Bravada to lie down and was able to rub her all over her back. Madelaine said she's been trying to do that with her since she first had her when she was 11 months old. She is now 12 years old.

The rituals may seem slow to some people but they work fast when you develop the bond as Madelaine discovered. Well done

The Gap Between Theoretical Training Methods and Practical Application

When training a horse, there is always a gap between the theoretical and the practical and this can be very frustrating. My advice for this is pretty much always that more time is needed. I can't overstate the beautiful simplicity of the first *Waterhole Ritual™* as a preparation for the rest.

So, this article features a question by one of my loyal readers Norman, who writes:

I have been having trouble with the Waterhole Rituals™. My horses just aren't reacting as I expected. During the first Ritual, my pony won't come up to me again after I move the chair away. I can't sneak up on any of them for the third Ritual. They always seem to be aware of everything around them. Should I chase them anyway? They never stop when I stop during the fourth Ritual. I don't know how long I should keep walking after them. I don't want them to resent me because I'm doing it wrong. Your Method is exactly what we need, it's just frustrating that I can't do it right.

Here was my reply:

In the beginning, your only problem is not taking the time it takes to achieve the desired response. The horses will respond to it but it will only happen when you take the time it's going to take.

The first *Waterhole Ritual™* is not about getting any interaction from your horse, it is about spending time with him. When sharing space the horse doesn't need to come back to you after moving your chair, it's not about the horse returning to you. Interaction is not part of *Sharing Territory* so what your horse is doing by not coming back to you is fine. Look at what the purpose of this Ritual is and continue to share space with your horse for 30 days before going on to the next Ritual. Each Ritual builds on the next, so you want to be sure that before going on to the next Ritual your horse is responding to the preceding one in the desired manner and that you can feel the connection growing with him. This will enable you to then see how the previous Ritual builds the opportunity to go on to the next.

On the *Leading from Behind* Ritual, just follow slowly behind the horse and eventually the horse is going to slow down and not feel the need to run away from you. When this happens and he does slow down enough, it will give you the opportunity to lead him from behind with an occasional urging him forward and following him just as is shown on the DVD. Don't urge the horse forward when leading from behind unless the horse stops and the energy is low. At this point, you can push gently, pause, push gently and then pause. This is about training a horse, a horse doesn't know unless you train him. I would also suggest a lot of the *Eye Contact* Ritual to slow your horse down.

If you are still having problems, I would like to suggest making an appointment for a phone consultation to talk with me directly. You can have an hour or a half hour phone consultation, which are followed by email follow-ups and the recordings of the calls so you can listen to them again and again. Students find this really beneficial. Hope that helps.

Training a Horse Using the *Waterhole Rituals™*

I recently had a letter from Helene in New York who was telling me about her attempts to get to know a large German warmblood that was recently bought by her barn owner. Helene freely admits she is only a novice horse rider and has no horse of her own but she wanted my feedback on her attempts to use the *Waterhole Rituals™* with this powerful horse.

We are kindred spirits and I am happy you enjoyed reading my book and blog. My advice is to stop your work with Max. I can see from your letter that you have a lot of talent for creative exploration and I would venture to say that you will be able to develop your skill with horses easily; however, you need more knowledge and horsemanship skill before you try to implement my Methods with Max. From what you are telling me about Max's background and your background, you are not a match. With Max, anyone would need complete understanding of my Method and success using it on horses that have no issues first. What you are attempting could be compared to trying to put a jigsaw puzzle together with your eyes closed except much harder because the puzzle is not dangerous and the pieces you are working with don't change shape. Max will present many behaviors and what will work with him in one minute would be inappropriate in another. Only after you have successfully worked with numerous horses that are appropriate to your skill level will you have the skill to handle Max.

My DVDs are designed for people who have a working understanding of horse behavior and for students that are working under my guidance or a qualified instructor in the *Waterhole Rituals™*.

My suggestion to you is to take the long journey if you love horses. Let horses and humans alike guide your way in more appropriate tasks. Learn to lead a smaller, more dependable horse through the *Waterhole Rituals™* rather than a big unpredictable horse you don't know, like Max. You require more knowledge under your belt before you start to experiment with horses as you have described.

I want to define leadership as it relates to horse training so everyone can understand why you need to take a slow approach relating to horses from the ground. You are the leader in the moment you give a request or suggestion in any form or even when you confine a horse in an area of your choosing. When a horse is in your hands you are taking full responsibility for his care, custody and behavior. You need to know how to read Max and how to bring a better connection and safety to you both. This takes time, and sharing space and doing nothing is what makes a really bond. It requires the "none action journey".

With my Method, the horse has no fault insurance. No chasing after a horse. It is so important to be able to communicate only in the moments of companion energy like you would with a three-year-old child. It would be a really good idea that when working at liberty you know how to keep the respect in place when the horse knows he is in control and wants to challenge you. Max did not want to be involved when you were chasing after him even if it looked like you were making progress. It is not a good idea to place your care in Max's hands and expect him to follow your lead. You are sending him a mixed message. You are saying *I am the leader and I do not know what I am doing*. That does not build trust with Max or give him a sensible reason that he should want to follow you.

In my Method I do not have my students chasing after horses, it breaks the trust. I always have food and water in the area in which I start my horse at liberty in and I do not start any interaction in the area until he feels this place is his home. This way I can communicate with him about territory issues to build a working bond.

First, you need to learn how to train, play, communicate, interact and click with horses in a free choice environment to learn the appropriate steps to take. Once you are able to handle easy horses, you then can work with a horse that might take more skill once you know the format. This way you will not lose your confidence, get hurt or injure your horse.

No horse is bad but we can surely develop bad acting horses and make them worse through trying to work with a horse we are not qualified to work with.

If Max was in my charge, I would be sitting with him daily for a couple of months or even longer before I tried to manipulate him in any way because he has had too much manipulation already. To start the relationship you want to create in him the desire to want your presence without interaction and to fall in love with you without food. You would need to make an everyday commitment as it is a lifestyle change using the *Waterhole Rituals™*. Horses need your companionship everyday when we keep them in captivity. I would suggest that you sit in a chair with Max for an hour a day doing nothing and at the same time, work with horses that are kid safe on the ground with a coach who knows my Method. Taking lessons along with sharing space while doing nothing is invaluable to developing your skill.

My book clearly points out how much time I spent before I took any interaction with the horses. What you are doing to this horse right now is a lot of manipulation that needs to stop. You are not courting your horse, though you might think you are. You need to let him court you and then know what you are doing.

I am not saying that you could not succeed doing what you are doing but the dangers are too many. I would almost never run from a horse or lead him to carrots before a horse will allow me to move him around with a reed easily. I never chase after a horse as you have described. In the beginning, I keep the horse in walk only.

The tip off that you are on the wrong track with your work at liberty is that you weren't sure of what to expect; Max was snorting and keeping an eye on you and you said that using a whip to drive him away or define your ground could possibly break the bond. This is not good news. In the beginning, this is too much speed, pressure and drama.

You need lessons with the reed before you use a whip. This way the whip will be accepted by the horse and he won't be afraid that you might hit him with it. Let me explain a little about how I use the reed. I must educate the horse to understand when I would like to touch him with it that he would not move away from it and would accept it as a grooming tool if that was my intention. He would understand that when I need him to move away, he would move away not from fear but from my request. I teach a horse to come to the reed, leave my company, go, turn, and stop. The reed and whip is not a tool of punishment but a guide; it is a direction tool and communication aid. The whip adds urgency to a request (not a demand) after the horse responds to reed.

It takes a lot of lessons and time around horses before you begin to take on an adventure such as the one you undertook with Max. It would be a good idea to first know how to develop a working bond in a 50 acre field that has other horses, pasture, food, carrots and water that you have no control of and learn how to school your horse in these conditions. The rules of working at liberty with my Method is that you only communicate with a horse when he comes to you; and when he leaves, you must leave him. From this rule, you garner the trust and bond faster.

This way of communication is very different to the way people go about training horses at liberty. I have used this rule for more years than I am going to mention and I still find it works like magic. You broke this rule when you were chasing after your horse. *Leading from Behind* or 'hazing' as I called it years ago is done when the horse wants to be with you, not when he wants to avoid you. If he should run away in this scenario, I just keep following after him in a slow ambling walk. This formula brings more trust and respect at the same time. If the slow ambling walk causes tension, I move on to something that would bring back the harmony and the return of the horse to my side.

I am concerned that you may do a large amount of damage to the good training that Max has retained and that could cause him to become aggressive in his defense. The safest way to be around a horse is in a large space and to stay in walk with companion energy and no chasing. To use the *Waterhole Rituals™* at this point, I would suggest that you find the right horse, a "Sweetie Pie" and sit in a chair and read a book. Share space with a horse that is kind and respectful in all circumstances until you have developed your skill. Wait till the "Sweetie Pie" comes up to you and wants to bond to you not the other way around.

Start with *Sharing Territory* and wait for this horse to come to you as a way to bond. When he becomes a nuisance, then move your chair or use your reed taking the space around him with swirling movements in the air around his body using your body language and your voice telling him he needs to leave. If you have done this properly, when he chooses to return he will not be so forward. After this action becomes a ritual to you both, you have the beginnings of a foundation. At that point you could leave and go get him a carrot and then go back to reading your book. Keep the carrots on the other side of the fence, not on you. You need to work with horses that appear to grasp the *Waterhole Rituals™* happily, quickly and naturally. This might take you some time to put together but you will grow much faster working with a horse that matches your ability to one that doesn't.

It is all about building relationship and understanding. Think of it this way; you can lead someone you trust and love to carrots more safely than trying to lead a thief you do not know to the carrots. Right now, you can't tell whether Max wants to be a thief or lover. Max has thrown all kinds of behaviors at you and we want to avoid this. I hope this open letter is of help to many of you who read my blog and who are working with my Method.

Is a Horse ever too Old to Start the *Waterhole Rituals™*?

A question from Becka in Washington

Is a horse ever too old to start Liberty Training? I recently pulled my young at heart 24 year old mare out of a lesson program. My goal was to give her a break from daily lessons and spend more time one on one with her. Unfortunately, my back problem prevents me from riding her. I am looking for other ways to enhance our relationship and develop activities we can do together. Liberty Training sounds perfect but I worry that she's too old and set in her ways to start something new like this. Is it worth trying? She's still quite responsive to direction, but also a bit set in her ways.

Here is what I wrote in reply to Becka:

I find that any age is fine for Liberty Training because it is what horses naturally do throughout their lives. Most importantly, change your presentation of the *Waterhole Rituals™* in the way that would bring about a positive result. The main thing is to focus on developing a bond by sharing space and developing trust by allowing your horse the ability to walk away from you when she needs to and to take her space away from her when she is not looking at you or when standing with her rump in your direction. If you have set food out for her, let her sometimes have control of the food as she eats when she keeps her eye on you and when asked to leave she would give up her food. Make these activities interesting, fun as well as challenging. After that, companion walking is natural.

When is it Time to Move to the Next Ritual?

Stephani from Florida wrote:

I have your Waterhole Rituals™ DVD. I am enjoying myself very much and my horse loves the first Ritual. What specifics do you look for that tells you that you are OK to start the next Ritual?

To which I replied:

When your horse is completely bonded with you and starts to become a pest. Before that, you could use the *Hello Ritual* to show your horse that when he walks away from you when you are approaching him, you will walk away from him. This way you build in your horse an understanding that he can get rid of your advances when he chooses, which will build more trust in him. He will feel that he can encourage your advances without the fear that he will lose control of his personal space. Every time you approach and leave will bring a deeper connection and develop a longing in your horse to know you better.

Interestingly, since Stephani sent in her question, she has obviously been watching the DVD and using the rituals more. She says that the first Ritual has been a real lesson in turning down her energy as she is normally a really dominant individual. She wrote:

Well Carolyn, I absolutely love your DVD. I am a very dominant type person - Type A personality and what I want - I go out and get - so to speak. Your DVD has helped me immensely in the regard to being a passive leader - one who requests and does not demand. My journey with horses is one that will benefit me, my family as well as my husband.

This is what I aim for in my work, to reach further than just working with horses. I would like to create a desire in individuals to have a need to serve community and a community that has a need to serve the individual. This applies to our families too of course. Well done, Stephani.

How to Approach and Leave Your Horse

I did a clinic a couple of months ago that we were recording for my latest DVD *Introduction to the Waterhole Rituals*™. I was working with the participants in the arena where we were all being horses and trainers.

I gave people a chance to work with me at liberty as if I was the horse and they were the trainer. This gave the students the possibility to move me around and find out how a horse would respond. This allowed the students to solve problems in a safe environment and then when they go back to work with their horses they would have a much clearer view on how to approach and how to leave a horse.

So anyway, this one girl was so cute. She was coming at me with the whip and I kept running away from her and she kept coming towards me. The problem was though, there was a fence right there and I had no place to go. Well, she cornered me up against the fence and the next thing you know, I found myself leaping out of the arena. Well, she looked at me so surprised because I was climbing out of the arena just like a little monkey trying to get out of there.

So I came back in and after we had done that exercise she said to me, "Gee, Carolyn, you didn't do that with anyone else, why did you do that with me? You didn't try to run away from other people". So, it's just really interesting how people can't understand that as long as you're approaching the horse, the horse has a desire to run away. All she needed to do was stop pressing me and back up and I wouldn't have had to jump out of the arena.

So remember, when you are pushing your horses, don't keep following after them if they're going very fast. All you have to do is back up.

Question About the *Say Hello* Ritual

Today we have a question from Michelle from Canada who is already using the *Waterhole Rituals™* to good effect by the sound of it but was seeking a little more clarification. Michelle wrote:

When I go to "Say Hello", Amber (my mare) will sometimes walk towards me, so do I retreat, continue and still walk off or what?? She also did this to me later on during the Eye Contact ritual, so I did some "Companion Walking" to compensate for her decision.

My response to Michelle was:

When Amber walks up to you, she is greeting you. She is in the driver's seat and she likes you. This is what we want to achieve using this Ritual. From this Ritual you want her to understand that your desire is to deepen the bond just like when people say "hello" and "how are you", to show that they care. The other part of this display is to point out to her that you respect her and that she is in charge of your advances and leadership.

You have achieved your goal as you have reported it to me. If she is a sweet horse, you can let her greet you. If she is more aggressive by nature, which I know she is not by how she is responding to the *Eye Contact* Ritual, when she approaches, you approach her faster using body language to suggest that she needs to stop her approach and with your voice, ask her to stop her movement forward. When she stops, walk up to greet her and walk away.

On the *Eye Contact* ceremony when she walks up to you, take her back to the food in *Companion Walking* and start over. She has her own style with these rituals. She is very smart. As long as she is responding by keeping an "eye on you", you are building her focus and again more respect as well as developing a greater right to lead her in her way of thinking. Forty-five minutes of eye contact in this manner or any other way of responding will increase her focus and I.Q.

Question Regarding *Companion Walking*

The question that you will find below comes from a lady called Michelle, who has a question that might be troubling some of you, especially if you are new to horses or have just started using my Method. Michelle writes:

In Companion Walking, does it matter which foot you use to step off with when you want her to move forward with you? Do you use the other foot when you want her to stay?

It does not matter which foot you use. Do not pay any attention to these details as it will restrict spontaneous expression in both you and your horse.

Question About the *Go Trot* Ritual

This article is another in the series of questions regarding my *Waterhole Rituals™*. Whilst the rituals look simple enough on the surface, there are levels of understanding and behavior beneath the surface that must be fully grasped before you can experience their full benefit. Nicole from Canada wrote in and asked me a couple of questions and we'll look at one of these today. I hope that you find it helpful to your understanding too.

I'm a friend of Liz Mitten-Ryan's and live near her. Liz and I were talking yesterday and I had some questions that she thought were interesting and that you might be able to help. So, here goes! I'll try to be as detailed as possible though I'm sure you won't need all the details to figure these questions out!

I'll ask the simpler question first. It has to do with 'Go Trot'. I've only been experimenting with this for 2-3 months but this is what's been happening. When I turn horses out after working/playing with them, or even when I do any liberty work in their paddock or pasture, I've been using two terms to 'release' them- "free" and "go play" to end our session and essentially telling them they no longer need to focus on me. However, I'm actually having trouble getting them to LEAVE! I take the halter off, give treats and scratches and then stand at their shoulder so they can clearly see me and with BIG body language tell them "FREE" or 'Go Play'... then I turn my back and leave but more often than not, they follow. So, I'm not clear in my body language or direction to them.

With 'Go Play' I usually use that when I'm coming back. I often do five minutes of liberty work, release them and come back ten minutes later. My goal is similar to what I've seen of your 'Go Trot'. I want them to leave with energy, and return with energy. This hasn't worked for me very well either. Sometimes they'll TEAR OFF towards their friends (not often, as I don't usually allow that kind of behavior) but most often the response I seem to get is a combination of surprise or even being startled when I send them away. Since I often need to snap the whip or use arm gestures, it is a surprise, but I can't get them to leave any other way!

My answer:

In answer to your questions regarding *Go Trot* at liberty, I want my horses to jump into a run when I say, *"Go trot"* but I do not surprise them. They may sometimes act surprised though and I like this kind of response because it gives me a great gas pedal. But before I would ask for this exuberant release, my horses should have a gas pedal that is completely under my control in that I can send them away in walk, trot or canter first.

To ask a horse to *Go Trot,* I do this. I ask them to stand and then when they do, I walk out of the heart area, pause and then say, *"Go trot."* If they do not go, I make a little stronger gesture and I back that up with a crack of the whip and step forward and direct them by pointing in the direction I would like them to go as a driving aid. If this does not work, they are not ready to do *Go Trot* yet. Whenever my horses do not perform, I change the subject and work on something I can get them to do happily. Before any direction takes place for this phase of the *Waterhole Rituals™* I must have the bond, the manners and extreme order with control first.

It might be a good idea that you work in the beginning in an area that your horse cannot graze in as a way to keep her interested. We want to make it as easy on you as possible in the beginning.

Before I ask for *Go Trot,* I have completed all the *Waterhole Rituals™* with my horse. I can tell that you have not. When I let my horses go after working them, I do not drive them away. What is the benefit of that? Always consider the benefits in what you are doing. I hang with them for a while and then I leave. I want to leave them feeling a connection with me in harmony so they are left with a good feeling rather than feeling dismissed. You say 'go play' but you are demanding that they play in an aggressive way. You would not speak to a three-year-old child in this way, so don't do this with your horses.

How to Avoid Behaving Like a Predator during the *Waterhole Rituals™*

Nicole's second question was *with regards to 'round penning'. I use quotes for this term because I seldom put a horse into a round pen for this work, more often it's in a two acre paddock with 3-4 horses. When I have a horse that does not come when called or leaves when I'm haltering, I will drive them off and separate them from their herd. I used to do this with a lot of energy and make them go at least at a trot, if not more. There would be lots of directional changes, both inward and outward turns. Then I would ask them to come back to me and most of the time they come running in.*

However, lately I've been feeling this is very 'rude' or aggressive and doesn't really honor the horse's free will ("come to me OR ELSE"). So, I've scaled it down to giving them time to come (I'll call several times, wait, change my position, etc) and if after 3-5 opportunities they still don't come, I drive them off at a walk.

Anyway, the whole point of this question is that when I separate them from the herd, keep them moving, or sometimes 'corner' them (from 50 feet away), some horses get very worried and I feel as though they see me as predator. Wouldn't a predator do the same thing? Separate the horse from the herd, chase them off to some corner or dead end and then GET THEM?! I know that lead mares discipline by kicking someone out of the group but do they continue to push them around?

My response was:

I do agree with you that you are behaving like a predator. I never corner my horses or drive them into submission. I want my horses to come up as fast as possible. The reason your horses appear aggressive in the call up is that you are not in control of their speed in the same way that you are not in control when asking them to leave you.

First, work my Method in walk, then trot, then walk and trot and then canter. Do not do this in a round pen in this stage of training because you do not have a clear bond. You need to have your horse in complete control at liberty first. I want you to have a connection with your horse like the boy in the 'Black Stallion' movie.

You are focused on the formula and not on the relationship. Your horses are not happy with your leadership and your choices. When you start with your horse always pick things that make you both happy. You are not doing the *Waterhole Rituals™* when you are focused on the performance. You can you have control of your horse without having to be controlling. Start training with a gentle attitude with lots of pauses.

My Method focuses on developing a working bond and the enthusiasm of the horse by increasing the bond, trust, respect as well as his focus and willingness. This is achieved by having your horse follow rules of herd behavior. When your horse does not do what you want, look at these possibilities:

1. You have not chosen the right thing to do with your horse; or
2. You are not clear in your direction; or
3. You are losing some quality of connection like trust, interest, respect; or

4. You are not preparing the horse to have the right energy for what you are asking them to do and, this is only because you have not seen my work yet

It sounds like you are taking too many shortcuts. Your mind is on control and training at the same time. We want to break it down for the horse so that we are either focused on control or training. In these moments, slow it down, get clear that there is no error on the horse's part and fall in love with your horse just as they are and take a break. Remember to train only when the horse is willing to listen and respond positively.

My suggestion is get rid of the roughness, strong direction and being demanding. Spend time doing the smallest of things. Be spontaneous like in my book, *Naked Liberty*. Be creative. Work on directing anti-social behavior in the moments the bond is vibrating deeply.

Read the chapter on page 178 of *Naked Liberty* about hanging out with your horse and practice reciprocal movements without expecting any performance. You need to sit with your horse every day for an hour to develop your skill with horses. The pause will bring you instant wisdom. It is the fastest education I can suggest.

When horses are made to perform, you appear to always have to make them, as opposed to getting a volunteered response. Horses always question dominant leadership. They never question a request if you have developed the relationship correctly. When you are training, the bond should be so deep that you need only to ask. Ask in harmony and unity and it is always given when the qualities are maintained through the *Waterhole Rituals™*.

If asking does not get the response you want, you need to return to developing the relationship and forget the training until you have order without the need for control through the rituals. You should only demand that the horse listen to your leadership when a herd rule is broken, never in riding and training should a horse experience a demand. Demands should only be addressed regarding territory rights and food issues.

Anytime you have to correct a broken law you need to love your horse afterwards until the horse feels connected again. Do a lot of fun things in between setting the rules around food. A second of correction and then a whole lot of loving until the horse is fine with the correction over the broken herd rule. You also really need to learn how to use a reed because your aids in leadership need to be effective and kind.

I hope this helps but if you are still struggling with this, may I suggest you set up a phone consultation with me.

A Journal of Ben's First *Waterhole Ritual™*

This is journal entry from Lori, who writes about her magical and unexpected experience using the *Waterhole Rituals™* for the first time with her horse Ben.

I worked with Ben today on the Waterhole Rituals™. Since this was going to be the first time for Ben, I lunged him first to make sure that his energy level was low and that he was warmed up if he wanted to run around when I turned him loose. Then I took the lead rope off and took some hay into the center of the ring. He began to eat. I walked around the arena for a while and then sat down in the sand to watch him. Of all of the horses I have dealt with he was the most calm but alert at the same time. He would intently look to see where I was from time to time and stop eating.

I thought I would play with this a little and worked on eye contact but very casually, maybe walking in a big circle around him once each way. Then I sat down maybe 15 to 20 feet away from him. He seemed completely relaxed as I was thinking about what I wanted to do next. I began by saying hello. Each time he would always pick his head up away from the food to say hello, being very respectful. I wanted to reward him for his close attention, so on about the third time, I gave him a small piece of carrot. He seemed content, and I walked away again. After about maybe four or five times, I thought about what I would do next and the only thing that seemed right was companion walking.

I had thought about trying to lead him from behind or taking his territory but it did not seem necessary and I thought that it might cause him to be afraid. I did move him off the hay once very gently and only a few steps to see how he would react to moving out of my space. I then called him back and he came back to the food. No big deal. I said hello again and petted him. I stood by his shoulder, clucked and asked him to walk and he did! It was so easy and has such a familiar feeling that I had to remember that I needed to get him back to the food quickly so that I could reward him for his behavior. I let him eat and we were off again! We had halt and walk and a slow trot with light encouragement that we did together. Unreal!

I felt almost in some weird way like I was cheating or not doing something right. However, I had never exposed this horse to the Carolyn Resnick Method before and it was awesome. I decided to take his halter off in case that made a difference. He liked 'naked liberty' just fine and did everything like he had been doing it for years.

I decided to work on "Go Trot and Come Up." This was more challenging because he was a little unsettled at first with being asked to leave me, so I started with first a few steps and then tried to bring him back. It took him a while to figure out that I wanted him to come in towards me when I called. After a few carrots, he got the message. We worked on both sides. After maybe 5-10 minutes, I could send him out in a small 10 -15 meter circle and he would come back in when I called. Then I asked him to stand while I walked away and then asked him to come up again. To me this is perhaps one of the best games to play with a horse. I think I must be easily entertained!

Since things were going so well, I decided to finish with a companion walk around the entire ring with halts occasionally. He felt like he had absolutely no desire to leave me. He was one of the most respectful horses of my space that I have ever worked with. He is good leading with a halter but not this good! I had no idea how this would go, I just knew I wanted to try him out. It felt so comfortable and relaxed and I am not sure I have ever used this word before but it was harmonious!

The other day Carolyn showed me Robyn Gate's video. It showed her walking her beautiful horse Cabo out of the gate and down the road for a wonderful hike through the wine country. Does it get any better than that? For the first time, I could really feel that this was obtainable. I remember commenting to Carolyn that it looks so natural that it almost looks normal but walking a horse with ease and without tack is definitely NOT NORMAL. Although for safety reasons I did not walk Ben back to his corral without a halter this time, I have every confidence that he would have. His halter had become a piece of horse fashion, not a tool, just something for looks. I'd better get him one in Coach leather and diamonds!

In reply I wrote:

How exciting! You developed a keen awareness in creating the right ingredients. I am so glad you are keeping a journal as many famous horse people have and do. It will be such good reference material for you and a gift for others who are using my Method.

Your awareness of how natural and connected you felt, and how you listened to your feelings and chose to present the rituals in a way that the horse could respond naturally to and want to connect with you without any drama was awesome. I like how you used my rituals creatively.

If you had been giving a clinic, you would have looked like a master of the equine bond and shape shifter of the dance.

I am so happy you have started working with my Method with other horses, this is how you grow. What you tapped into was the tendency of the horse and you did a good job of that. Now you must continue doing the same things with him until it becomes habitual and less conditional. Good luck!

You need to sit with your horse for thirty minutes on regular basis to allow you and your horse to make a real connection before the interactions. You need to get your horse to see that when he is turned loose in the arena he needs to relax and you could get this across to him by holding a rope and sitting in a chair in the arena while he is eating. I would not have chosen to lunge my horse but I was happy to see you choose that route for yourself because it shows you were thinking ahead and it worked for you.

Spending time sharing companionship doing nothing, reading a book, or writing a journal builds a trust that you need to acquire. I am not talking about a blind trust, but another kind of trust that makes perfect decisions in all circumstances. It opens the attitude of the horse to see you as a family member, which will bring out his desire to communicate with you naturally. This way you can tap into a universal language that all living creatures understand. Sharing time and space with your horse in the moments will enable you to tap into this zone of connection, communication, clarity and knowingness.

If you enjoy the pause, you will receive knowledge that cannot be acquired in any other way. The bond must be developed in the pause. There are all kinds of bonds and the bond you are working on is a bond that is not conditional. Just know that this kind of bond, no matter how unconditional it becomes, still needs to be maintained. You now know that the magic between horses and humans is truly not imaginary.

Now you can settle down for the long journey. I know that you are very gifted and the journey you take will always be on the cutting edge of discovery. You can see clearly now the right direction to take your understanding of how to use my Method. People think that when the bond is established they do not need to maintain, fix or adjust the connection and the relationship, and that is why marriages get into trouble.

LIBERTY TRAINING

Dangers of Working a Horse at Liberty

In this day and age it's great to take advantage of the ability we have to share YouTube videos with each other. It is a wonderful tool I can use to guide you in how the connection looks, how to lead a horse through the *Waterhole Rituals™* and what the result looks like. It is also very nice to have the support of my students sharing their perfect connection with their horses.

As this new way of sharing information unfolds, I want to call attention to the dangers of working a horse at liberty. The reason I what to do this is some people can make the mistake of doing things that are not safe. Some think that sharing a heart connection and being on a spiritual journey buys them some form of protection and magic and that they can therefore forget the dangers of working around and with a horse at liberty.

Horses at liberty can be more dangerous than they are with tack because of their natural self-expression (sudden movements, biting, kicking, etc.) and their understanding that they are free to express themselves. A horse interacting with you as he would another horse could result in an accident. Horses are aggressive around food with each other, they commonly run into and through one another. Horses can be aggressive or fearful which can bring a defensive response, or they can lose focus. All these conditions are not good if you don't know how to choose the approach and correct positioning that will keep you safe.

Some people make the mistake of thinking that their horse is following their lead and they see the horse as playful in its expression when the opposite is true; the horse is acting in an aggressive manner but hasn't turned up the volume yet.

Working with the *Waterhole Rituals™* requires a certain consciousness to stay safe and a well-rounded knowledge of horse behaviour, as well as lessons in Liberty Training. Yes, many people are getting great results with my Method and that is why it can be so exciting. But a little bit of knowledge and having instant success with my Method can be misunderstood. It is not a quick fix, but rather a long journey to mature a spiritual connection with your horse, and it is a way to develop partnership and performance. The skills needed are leadership, and an ability to solve problems. If you do not know how to lead a horse, the rituals will not be effective in any way except where leadership is not required such as with first two rituals. Once you have a connection though the *Waterhole Rituals™*everything can fall apart from not knowing how to lead and maintain trust and respect. To maintain it, you need to recognize what your horse is consistently thinking throughout the work session.

Even though the *Waterhole Rituals™* are easy to learn, for many people it really needs to be something you learn from a qualified person so you do not make mistakes about your horse's level of respect for you. Some YouTube videos on my Method are not representative of a responsible approach and can cause great error in judgment and a complete misunderstanding between you and the horse. When deciding whether a person has the skill to work with my Method, my rule of thumb is that they should be able to keep a well trained horse well trained and manageable, and they also need to have natural leadership abilities in general.

Importance of Natural Leadership Ability when Working at Liberty

Let me explain what I mean about having natural leadership ability and the importance of this when working at liberty.

Someone called me and asked if they could get any benefit training their horse with my system from watching the DVDs alone even though they did not have previous horse experience. So I asked him some questions and from his answers I felt safe to say I thought that in his case, the DVD would be of some benefit although I could not be sure of that. It turned out that the DVDs were helpful and did the trick for him. He got all his stallions trained.

The questions I asked were:

- Do you have a well trained dog? (It turned out he had a dog and a cat)
- Does the dog behave in the house?
- Does the cat not claw the furniture?
- Does your wife love and respect you and do your children honor you and did they grow up independent and happy and able to fit into society and serve the community?

He answered "yes" to all these questions and that let me know he had the basic skills needed in life. He made the choices in leadership that create order, harmony and respect. He did not even think that my questions were strange and that was a tip to me that he knew what he needed to have to be able to make good leadership choices with horses. What I understood from his answers was that his assessments on how to lead and support were all in place.

Robin Gates, one of my students and an instructor of my Methods, can be seen on YouTube working with different horses. What you see Robin doing looks simple but takes years of practice. My aim is to inspire people to see the benefit and take the long journey to become a student in learning my Method. The practice of the *Waterhole Rituals™* is life-changing and brings a great spiritual understanding and personal empowerment from learning the art of connection and leadership. It is very important to know what you know and know what you don't know.

This will keep you safe and help you make the right choices to gain a magical connection with your horse.

What is important to understand is that if you cannot clearly understand the purpose of each Ritual and how you would use it to get a desired response from your horse it is better to take lessons and not try to carry on by yourself with them. If the rituals do not work easily for you, stop and seek lessons with a qualified instructor like myself or Robin.

Sending a Horse Away at Liberty

I want to address a problem that people are having sending a horse away from them at liberty. Many people have expressed concern that driving a horse away from them will hurt the trust and bond. I can understand this point of view because of the struggle it might take in their mind to teach a horse to leave you when he does not want to go.

But it is a very simple fix and I am surprised that someone who is having this problem has not figured it out. First, I want to say that for a horse not to leave you when you ask him to is a big problem if you are planning to use my Method because it requires the ability to move a horse quickly or slowly and at any speed you ask, going away or returning.

If horses are left to their own nature, they will usually not be difficult to move away from you if you ask them to. This lack of ability a horse has to want to leave you is a learned behavior. It is generally caused by desensitizing the horse to movements around their personal space and this creates a horse that will not respond to your body language and your intent. The horse becomes completely non-observant.

I want to point out why some people are looking for a method to solve their problems rather than figuring it out for themselves. They are focused on training methods for their answers rather than looking for a creative solution. I want to build in my readers a leadership that has creativity, planning, and humanity.

I really valued Kate from the NW's comment to my blog entry *A Lesson on How to Create a Better Connection with a Horse*. I thought it showed very creative problem solving that allows her to be a leader to her horse and move the relationship forward. It is an example of creativity, planning and humanity in her ability to be a leader by reading the information on my blog and applying it to her situation.

I want to show you how to empower your leadership and problem solving skills. The first thing that is important about a method for training a horse is not the "how to" part. What is important is to look closely at the method to understand what the horse needs to learn from it. Then it is up to you to develop a plan that suits your horse and your philosophy. Coming at methods from this point of view makes for an easy solution. Of course, the thing to remember when training a horse is one must have some experience with horses to train them. There is a simple test to see if you qualify to have the skill necessary to train a horse.

Can you keep a good horse good and not take the good training out of him? If you can do that you qualify because every time you interact with a horse you are essentially training him even if you had no interest in the matter. Every time we connect with a horse, we influence his attitude and behavior for the next time he gets used.

This is why when someone buys a horse the horse can get better or worse. Because horses are prey animals, they spend their lives adjusting and making changes in how to respond to their environment, each other, and to you.

When a horse cannot be made to leave your company, this is an artificially learned behavior. Wild horses that bond with people do not have any problems responding to being moved away and coming back, because their nature has not been erased out of them through training in a way that would wash away the instinct to bond and fit in with herd dynamics and taking directions.

We must be careful in seeing the consequences of the training we put into horses and the problems we can cause training certain behaviors, like bomb proofing or stick with me. Most of the problems we create come from how we go about domesticating horses and how we go about training. Many people have no problem at all getting a horse to run away from them in fear but then the horse has no interest in coming back. Others cannot get their horses to move at all no matter how much they work at it, because they have spent too much time and energy on bomb proofing, or bonding with treats or whatever other interactions that have built the behavior.

Training a Horse Using Liberty

Today we have a question from Victoria in Australia who writes

I have a 9 year old thoroughbred mare, who I bought as a green, broken four year old. I trained her up for show jumping and she was coming along quite well until she fractured her offside hind when she was seven. Since then she has had problems on and off with lameness and more recently a sore back. She is perfectly capable of movement in the paddock but is uncomfortable and sore with a rider. The vets are unable to help anymore. So I have decided to take a new track with her and train her in liberty.

I have had experience in some well known natural horsemanship methods and have not found them useful as they seem to base their ideas on a horse that is scared of people. My horse and I are friends. I would just like to still be able to teach her new things to keep her mind occupied and so we can keep having fun together. I was wondering if you had some ideas of basic tricks I could teach her. Thanks for your help.

I wrote back:

Try teaching her to go away, disconnect from you and come back to you when you call her. If she goes a good distance from you, she does not have to disconnect, you can just call her back. What you do not want is for her to be in charge of how far she is to go. This could be easy for you since she is a good friend.

You start this interaction by giving her lots of treats, and then ask her to go trot or walk and when she returns on your call, she gets another treat. At first, it will be a little hard to get her to go, which is where the training comes into play as both you and your horse develop good team working skills. You may have to teach her how not to eat the treat first before you start this game, and that you are in control of the treats and she is not!

Once you can send her away and call her back, try sending her to a friend. When she waits politely with the friend she gets a treat from her as well. Then have your friend send her back to you as you call her at the same time. You now are having a good game of Horse Tennis. You can do this back and forth at walk and trot. All this teaches a horse that it is fun to be with all people in general. At the same time, she learns and exercises proper behavior around treats and she develops great relationships, and polite social conduct interacting with humans. This exercise helps a horse to feel responsible for their conduct and their performance.

Stina's Views on Liberty training

The wonderful thing about the internet is that you can reach people all across the world and never have to leave home. Stina, who is Norwegian but lives on the island of St. Vincent in the Caribbean, is a friend and student. Stina got in touch with me towards the end of 2007 and I started coaching her by phone and email. The results for her and her herd of wild horses have been astonishing, for which I must give Stina huge credit.

Stina was recently featured in *Hesteliv*, the main horse magazine in Norway. The magazine interviewed four Norwegian horse trainers including Stina and I thought it would be fun to show it to you and to read what Stina had to say.

Do you think that we are seeing more interest and a change in approach towards how we keep and handle horses using more "alternative methods"?

Yes, absolutely. More and more people can see how much we can learn from the horse. The horse is not just there for us, it has a much bigger meaning. I think many people have been in my situation, where they start to ask questions about why we should "fight" with our horses. When I took dressage lessons, the teacher told me to pull the reins harder so as to keep the horse's head down. My arms were already tired; there was no logic to it. If a horse can feel a fly on its rear leg, which it can then gently sweep away with its tail, why should I have to tire out my arms to make the horse do what I want?. Later on, I got a mare which I looked forward to be with every day but she was not happy with me at all.

This signalled the start of a journey for Stina and after many courses, seminars and discussions, her path changed. New riding improved her seat; she changed the tack, dental care and food, as well as taking the horse's shoes off and keeping him outside with the other horses 24/7. Slowly, Stina could see her horse change from being unhappy and shut down to happy and energetic.

I think many people are looking for a good connection with their horse. They want their horse to speak to them and come to them in the paddock and to like the training they do and the goals they want to achieve. Many are looking for new methods to achieve happiness and find a good energy in cooperation with their horse. I think it is important to let people know that is it not so difficult to get this. But this depends on the rider/owner understanding the nature of the horse and deciding to learn new things.

It was a big challenge for me to train the herd of wild horses in the Caribbean, an almost "impossible" task but I wanted to find a method and a way to solve it. I thought I was pretty good with horses and had quite a lot of knowledge, but no, it did not work on these horses. So I went back to school after getting in contact with Carolyn Resnick and it has been very exciting.

Inspiring Ways of using Liberty Training

I have a student I want to tell you about today because she has used my Method in an interesting way and it might help or inspire others to use it this way. To give you some history she once had many horses of her own and ran a successful riding, training and equine therapy business. Since she shut down her business and was without horses, an opportunity presented itself years later to help a stranger with an Icelandic Pony in need of attention.

When she arrived at the farm, she said she was immediately disappointed. She had hoped that there would be a space large enough to practice my Liberty Method. But, the pony was cute and she could tell that she needed him as much as he needed her, so they began their journey. At first, she just sat in his small pen and practiced the first ritual, *Sharing Territory*. This was something she said she found difficult to do at first even though it is a simple task. What was hard for her was to do nothing at all but connect to herself and act disinterested in the pony.

That is after all why she was there, to "DO" something with the pony. But she sat with him five days a week for an hour or so each day for several months as there was no place to go and do the liberty work that she was interested in and she discovered the pony was very ill. Since the space available was so limited, when they did go outside the pen she used my *Uberstreichen* exercises to begin developing a bond and respect.

Blaise, the pony, had foundered and it was later discovered that he had Cushing's. This became increasingly troubling to her as Blaise was in a significant amount of pain and all she could do was sit there with him. During that time she said something interesting happened. She started noticing his attention frequently turned towards her and during the time she sat with him he would stand beside her and they would play little games. These games were just simple interactions like touching him lightly on his chest to see what the least amount of pressure was that would cause him to back up. She then created a signal that brought him forward to come back to her. She became aware of the connection and communication that was available and present.

Much of her time was spent touching him eventually finding all the spots he enjoyed and assisting him in any way to feel better. She showed up one day and he was lying down in pain, which she had noticed had increased and the inflammation in his feet was causing him great distress. She sat with him for a while and then lay down beside him sharing that space with great concern. During this time he was seen and treated by a vet and began to stabilize.

When he was able to walk without pain, she took him on short walks off the property. One day she noticed that there was a house nearby that had two horses in the backyard. As she passed the house, she said the pony "told" her he wanted friends and indicated he wanted to enter the property. As it had a gate, my student "said" to the pony that she understood his communication but she had to follow human rules. She would need permission before entering. This seemed to satisfy him and later with permission to visit, they discovered the perfect place for liberty was next door!

In a very short time, they worked their way through the *Waterhole Rituals™* creating a deep bond and connection. Their journey continues, and she continues to keep me up to date on the relationship as it develops. What I want to share is that many people focus on horses that are healthy, fit, athletic, etc. This is a great example of how my Method can give well being and joy to any horse regardless of circumstances. How nice for this pony to have a relationship and connection that provides a feeling of belonging and being led, of connection and being understood.

Also, it may be that the time that she spent with the pony created a miracle. In the Spring the pony shed out his coat which is a sign that he doesn't have Cushing's so either there was a miracle or a misdiagnosis but either way I believe that attentiveness can create miracles like this.

Liberty Training in Nature

Margaret wrote: *I have just read your book and loved it. I've been ploughing through various horse training methods and ideas with some positive outcomes but not without feeling like a perfectionist, pushing up the pressure in getting the job done. I was left with a feeling of anxiety every time I went to work with a horse. I read "One with the Herd" which led me next to your book and related to it in wanting that bond and willingness with my horse without all the demanding and "correcting".*

I've been working with my horse and our bond has been developing so naturally. We were doing great at our little ground work lessons at liberty as well as our halterless hikes through the woods (Autumn's a one and a half year old 16 hand Belgian filly). For the past few months, I have had her out with a herd of 30 horses on 230 acres set in the redwoods on the side of a mountain, where she drinks from ponds and grazes on the meadows. It's a tame wild for those horses. Anyhow, she'll come up to me to say "Hi" and will sometimes stay but other times she'll just take off.

What can I say, it hurts my feelings. She hasn't wanted to do our liberty exercises or hikes. I feel that now she is more in with the herd, the less she feels the need to be around me. I just wonder if it's because she's young or I'm not stimulating enough, or she's just herd bound. I don't know if leaving it up to her liberty to follow me and want to do some things is right. I don't know. Should I just hang out with her more in the pasture and wait longer for her to initiate something? I give her lots of time but I'd hate her just to lose interest in me all together. I was just wondering if you had any insight. I just want to have the best relationship with her that I can. Maybe I just need to chill out.

In response I replied:

Margaret, you are very lucky to have this opportunity. Horses prefer being with horses in the wild. The carrot of freedom and self-direction and community of the herd is stronger than anything you have to offer her at this time. I would not feel hurt but rather be overjoyed that I could give my horse this lifestyle. I would suggest that you join her instead of her joining you so you can understand her life and what it will take to redirect her focus. Let these conditions take over your focus and be with your horse on her terms. You are lucky to have such an environment even for yourself.

Take this opportunity to fall in love with nature, discover how to be in the moment and at peace with what is. Become aware of the system in nature and the community of the herd. Become a wildlife lover and enjoy her experience. Take pictures and groom her when she itches. Bring her food like alfalfa and wait for her to finish it. When she finishes it, follow her if you can. Go with her if she will let you. Pay attention to the distance she would like you to keep.

Why is it that she must follow your lead for you to feel good about the connection you share with her? She might have the same feeling you do. She might say, "Why is it that to have a bond with Margaret I must go where she goes?"

Enjoy the time that you have to fall in love with the relationship as it is. I could give you a method to connect with her in the wild but it would be, in my mind, not to your best interest or hers. If you become one with her in her freedom you can better understand her point of view and then when her point of view does not hurt your feelings, you will be better equipped to make choices to empower your leadership.

Again you and your horse are very lucky to have the environment you have. By the way, get to know the other horses too. Take a chair to the place where they go most often, sit in the chair and read. If the horses come up to you, ignore them unless they get pushy and if they get pushy, move or ask them to leave you alone by using your body language to drive them from your personal space. Give the horses freedom to inspect you. This creates trust and increases the bond. Have fun with nature as it is.

Keep all of us informed of your journey getting to know the true nature of horses. I think it is most important that you stop looking for formulas at this point. Let the experience in nature open up your possibilities. If you do, I will offer you guidance along the way. Remember, your horse is quite young so what's the hurry? How much time do you give your horse on a daily basis? I hope enough to be able to grow the connection naturally.

CHAPTER FIVE
SOLVING TRAINING PROBLEMS

STRATEGIES FOR OVERCOMING RESISTANCE

Getting a Horse Present and Connected to Overcome Resistance

Last week I gave a lesson to a student of mine, Stephanie, who has a Welsh Cob mare that she has been driving and riding. The horse is very fearful and so she had started doing the *Uberstreichen Exercises* and working on getting her comfortable in her territory.

The problem I noticed with this mare was that although she was doing well with the *Waterhole Rituals™*, when she was brought to the barn, she did not want to have the bridle put on her. She was acting sort of wild and frightened, so I asked how long this had been going on. Stephanie said it had been like this for a long time. I told her that we had to get the horse comfortable with being present right there and right then, and to get her to agree to the fact that she likes being at the barn before we even attempt to put on the bridle.

So I took the horse and I asked her to stand still on one spot. Now, what people often fail to understand is how definite I am about where I want the horse to stand. I'm not talking about standing in the general vicinity of a spot, I'm talking about standing on the exact spot that you have chosen. So much so in fact, that if the horse steps off a quarter of an inch, you make her pick up her foot and put it back on the exact same spot.

Well, we did that with this mare once and it changed the whole performance. The next day Stephanie called me and said, "I can't believe how that horse has changed!" She told me that she took her out of her paddock, brought her up to the barn and was very clear about having her stand on one spot. Then after a while, she was able to put on the bridle with no trouble whatsoever. The horse wasn't concerned about being at the barn and did not shy like she used to, because Stephanie was able to get the horse to become present and connected in one place and in the moment.

Try this for yourself if you are experiencing similar challenges, with or without your horse.

Change the Frame of a Horses Mind to Overcome Resistance

The story I'm about to share with you will be practical information for those of you who really know how to use the *Waterhole Rituals* ™and who have trained a few horses with them. For those of you that haven't, let it be "food for thought" for the future as you grow as horsemen and women. I want people to think about what is going on in their horse's mind. No one should try the strategy I am going to share with you unless they are expert trainers with my Method or can see how it would work perfectly with the horse they plan to use it on.

This is how the training session went. Robin Gates, one of my Certified Instructors, was working for the first time with a mare that had training issues and she had been hired to bring out a better attitude and willingness in the mare. She started with the Ritual *"Sharing Territory (in Companionship)"* at liberty and got a connection with the mare. Once the connection was made, she asked for a simple request but the mare's outburst said clearly, "I do not like what you asking of me." Then the mare ran off to the far corner of the arena to pout. Robin went down to the end of the arena where the mare was, walked up to her and said "Good girl", patted her and fed her a cookie.

The mare repeated this behavior several more times. Robin told me that the mare clearly did not like that she could not get Robin to take any notice of her resistance. But finally, the mare gave up and started enjoying the cookies she was being fed. Once she became less resistant, Robin started taking charge. When the mare came to Robin for more cookies, Robin told her that she needed to go back to that same spot that she first fed the cookies to her. Robin then continued to create more rules about where the mare needed to be to eat the cookies and in due time the mare worked easily at liberty and loved Robin and the program. Her whole mood changed to being soft, willing and happy.

By not addressing the resistance¸ Robin shortened the time it took to train the horse. In no time, the mare could fully be directed in a willing state without the need for cookies. If you take time to put a horse into a schooling frame of mind without force, you will be able to use any method of training to its best advantage.

That night when she went to bed, Robin could not sleep because she was so excited and elated from the training session she had experienced with this mare. When the mare started out, she had been like a sullen teenager going on a dreaded vacation with her parents. Yet later on in the session, she was working in a precise manner and with a willing attitude. Robin was able to win her over by 'rewarding' the resistance with a cookie and then methodically easing her back into connection and responsibility through giving her challenges that won her over. This approach of giving cookies for resistance could have easily met with more resistance but it is where Robin put her focus that caused the strategy to work.

Understanding the Nature and Mind of Horses

I have already told the story of how my long-time friend and Certified Trainer, Robin Gates, overcame resistance with a horse she was training. For what it's worth then, here is my opinion on how Robin viewed and dealt with the situation.

To get the performance and respect from a horse, you need to understand the mind and nature of horses and figure out what would work with that horse in that moment of time. You will also always come up with a better strategy coming from a place of unconditional love and connection rather than wanting to lay the law down as soon as you've got the horse in a good mood. In other words, you can lay down the law better with an open heart!

On the other hand, one sure way for failure is to take the love too far and expect the strategy to work by showing the horse too good a time, thinking that the respect and responsibility will follow naturally. Most likely the horse will be less responsible because you did not create the necessary requirements to build responsibility and willingness in your horse.

Do not depend upon a formula alone to work for you without all these considerations. If you listen to that smart side of your nature and understand all that, then the right strategy comes naturally.

It's about focusing on the relationship not on the method, and this is exactly what Robin did. Remember, you can get many different results using the same strategy. When a horse shies on a trail, a pat could reassure a horse and stop the horse from shying or teach a horse to shy because he thought he was being praised for shying. Always, it is how the horse perceives your communication that will give you the results you get. It is very important therefore to feel the vibration of the horse and allow the vibration of the horse to direct your next move.

The 4-step formula on how to develop your strategy in training horses:

- Work on the basis of unconditional love and your need for respect and performance;
- Listen to your better judgment;
- Look at all the possibilities and have alternative plans;
- Work with your horse on what fits his abilities and broadens his well-being.

From this point of view, you can be the magic behind any method you use IF (this is a big if) you understand the nature of horses. It is important to understand that there is a lot of planning and adjustment to be made in leadership to build a proper connection with a horse after the cookie is eaten.

Simple Things Can Work Wonders

Sometimes the simple things work wonders with horses. This is another story I want to share with you about how I caught a horse that was uncatchable. It was during my first job in La Jolla, California where I was hired to handle a large training center of hunters and jumpers. What they like to do in some of these training centers is to play a little joke on you on the first day that you arrive. It's a way of breaking ice and getting to know you a bit better through laughing together. This is really important when somebody is hired to be the leader and I was hired to manage the whole ranch, so I had several trainers under my care plus many, many horses in training.

Anyway, they gave me a job to go out into a field and get this mare called Misty. They said to bring her in, groom her, and medicate her foot as she had a bad foot. So I went out and got her, brought her in and medicated her foot. However, whilst she was in the cross-ties, she almost killed me! I was on her right side, grooming her, little knowing that she had developed a habit or little trick of her own, which was to try and slam people up against the wall with her body as hard as she could.

Well, she tried this on me but as luck would have it, I somehow managed to avoid the blow, which was just as well as I cannot even begin to imagine the damage that she would have done to my body if she had succeeded.

As you can imagine, I was really unhappy with the people at the center because they must have known about this habit and I could not believe that they would pull such a trick on me. So, I went to the man who had hired me and I was really livid. I said, "How could you do that to a human being? I could have been killed!"

He said, "Wait a minute, you got Misty out of the field?" And I said, "Yes." He said, "Oh! I had no idea that you were going to get that far with her. She's been out in that field for three years and nobody has ever caught her. We've been out there with up to 10 people but she always got away from us. How on earth did you ever get a halter on that mare?" he asked.

"Well, that's interesting," I said. I think he was expecting me to go into great detail about what I'd done and the brilliant horsemanship skills I must have used. I went on, "As I was approaching the field she was in, I called her name and she just ran down and put her head on the outside of the fence. So I put the halter on her without even entering the field, then just opened the gate and walked her out."

She was actually the easiest horse I have ever caught out in a field. I did not have a grain bucket with me or anything. So, it is just really interesting that nobody ever thought of just calling her name. So I guess the moral to this story is always try the simple, obvious things first before going on to something else.

Training a *Stubborn* Horse!

This question comes from Melissa in Indiana and is typical of ones like this that I receive on a regular basis. Her situation involves a horse that is just too bossy! Perhaps this sounds familiar to you too? Melissa writes:

I have a 4.5 year old gelding quarter mix I've had since he was seven months old. He has had 45 days professional (natural horsemanship) training and that was almost two years ago. I know that's not much and

I'm at fault for him being so pushy because I do not put enough time in saddle!

I just find I'm more easily intimidated and less confident riding since having kids. Very common I'm told. I really want to ride but its more work and aggravation than fun riding him because he's very pushy, bossy and stubborn! I wanted to send him back this spring for a refresher, however I'm not comfortable with other local trainers in our area because there are not a lot of good stories from fellow horseman; there is a lot of bullying and cowboy riding.

I can't bring myself to get off my butt to work with him on a regular basis. There's no excuse but what do you suggest I do without spending a fortune or getting a broken bone from getting bucked off?

What I wrote to her: TAKING TERRITORY

I recommend you slow down and get into a connected relationship with your horse; that is, a relationship based on understanding what he is really seeking, which is leadership. If you read my book and watch my DVD about the *Waterhole Rituals™*, you will see that there is a relationship built on connecting to the very heart of the horse that will solve many of your problems. It does not allow the horse to be bossy or pushy, and it is simple to do.

The first thing I recommend you do is spend some time with your horse at liberty in his pen. Take a 5' flexible reed or stick, one that is very light or you can use a very soft whip. Your intention is not to disturb your horse or frighten him. You will walk slowly around the pen away from your horse, slowly moving the reed right and left with the reed pointed down at the ground. Then turn toward him and slowly approach. As soon as he moves away from you, you are to turn and move away from him. Repeat this a number of times until you are seeing your horse respond to the lightest suggestion to move away.

This will give you your horse's respect. It puts you in a leadership position. You are declaring your leadership in your horse's eyes by taking territory. If your horse becomes panicked or too defensive, then you may need to work with someone who has been trained in my Method.

Keep your horse company by sitting in a chair in his pen and read a book. If he approaches and you feel safe and comfortable, then let him stay close to you. If he is bothering you or if he is too aggressive, then ask him to move away from you. If he is sensitive, then you can move away from him by picking up the chair and sitting elsewhere.

These exercises will create a closer bond with respect. Plus, they are fun and enjoyable!

DEALING WITH FEARFUL HORSES

Fearful to dependable

Here is an exciting YouTube video clip by Robin Gates, a certified coach in my Method and student over many years. I am highlighting this clip because it shows the results of building a partnership from the ground using the *Waterhole Rituals™* and how effective it is with warmblood horses to develop trust and a working bond.

In the clip, you can see that Paulo has developed a wonderful gas pedal and brake; a great connection with Robin and a wonderful work ethic in full focus and he has an undeniably enthusiastic nature. His ears are not back and he is relaxed and forward. The connection that Robin gained with the *Waterhole Rituals™* translates to the saddle with the same integrity.

Paulo was once a very fearful horse, difficult to manage, overly spirited and could really intimidate people easily. He had been to one very good trainer, who after several months said that he was getting worse. Warmbloods can be very difficult sometimes on these points. When Robin got him, she said that he was completely unmanageable and only focused on wanting to get back to the herd. She pointed out that Paulo had been raised well without any abuse. After Robin had trained Paulo with the *Waterhole Rituals™*, he turned out to be a dependable horse under saddle as a jumper for his owner.

I frequently see how the most difficult horses can become the most dependable when corrected with the *Waterhole Rituals™*. I want to emphasize that it takes the skill of a qualified master or talented novice in the Method to do this kind of training with a difficult horse and it should not be attempted by someone without the proper skill set.

When you first use the *Waterhole Rituals™* use them on a horse that is kind and willing, easy to get along with so that the relationship and the skills in training can progress effortlessly. Just like when a person begins to learn how to ride, they don't pick a horse that lacks training or a desire to be ridden as the horse to learn on.

Horse Shying and How to Deal With It

Today, I would like to talk to you about why horses shy. I am sure a lot of people would like some idea of why this can happen. There are of course many reasons why a horse shies, and it is sometimes very complicated to say exactly what it is. Many times, however, the horse shies because something spooks him and he wants to get back some control. So instead of performing the act that he is being asked to, he shies. In those circumstances, the best way to get over it is opposite to what most people do. The traditional thing to do is try to get the horse used to the object in question. Instead, try this. Ride your horse past the object, do not pay any attention to it and continue on your way. This way gets the horse over the idea that he needs to control the situation.

Another reason that a horse might shy is because he is afraid of having you on his back. So the best thing to do is to work with him from the ground and get the horse to understand you better and accept your leadership using the *Waterhole Rituals™*. I know my own horses would never think about shying with me but would shy with a stranger. The reason is that a stranger would not have good leadership ability with my horses, so the bond of trust would not be there.

I had one woman at a horse training seminar with me that always suffered from her horse shying. The problem was that every time her horse would shy on the trail, she would pat him and say, "Good boy, it's OK." Well, that caused that horse to become the biggest shying horse I ever saw in my life, because he just wanted to be patted and told that he was a good boy and you can't blame him!

So when I'm out there riding the trail and my horse becomes nervous, I will sometimes take the alternative approach and just ride him home again. Once there though, I will turn around and ride him out again to the same point that he was nervous before. If he starts to get nervous again, I ride him back home again and back again and keep doing this until he will go down the road quietly enough.

Be More Tender With Your Horses

The story that I would like to share with you today is something that happened to me a couple of weeks ago when we were doing some filming. We were working on my new DVD that we are going to be bringing out showing the different personalities of horses and how each personality responds to the *Waterhole Rituals™*.

We had a horse there that is known as a fearful, shy horse and we needed to film one like that, to not only show his experience with the rituals but to show people what a fearful horse looks like. When we got the horse, I started to take him away from his buddy and down to the arena where we were going to be doing the filming. The horse was so fearful that it was clear it was going to be very traumatic for both of us just to get him down there.

So I thought before we start, I'd better develop a better relationship with him in order to make it easier on him. First off, I thought I'd take him to the barn and let him have some grain but when we got there, he was so fearful he could not eat. So I took him back to his buddy and once more he started to settle down.

My next thought was that I could lead him back to the barn again since he would remember the last time this happened and that it was OK because when he did this he got to see his buddy again. Well, I did that and that didn't work. So then I got a bucket, put some grain in it and took him to where he could see his buddy and let him eat out of the bucket. In a short time, this horse figured out that I was working with him and I was eventually able to lead him away from his buddy and let him eat at the barn where he could not see his buddy anymore.

I did not get him to the arena that day but we did make big inroads with him. I will still have a horse that we can film and show fear but at least we will both feeling much better about it when we do that filming.

So the reason I am sharing this story is that I want people to be a little more tender with their horses and maybe figure out ways that they could get their horse to feel better about what they are going to ask them to do.

Being Present in the Moment

Here we are into another day and I have just finished working with my horses once again. I have been working with that fearful horse I was telling you about; the one I was taking from his buddy and his paddock to the barn and feeding him grain.

Well, he is doing really, really well. Now I can take him out of his paddock to the barn, and I don't have to bring him back to his buddy anymore. He is happy to be with me and is learning a lot of new things. One of the things I have taught him is how to travel with his head really low.

He learned that surprisingly fast, although when I started with him he was really unsure about doing it. I fixed the problem, however, with the *Uberstreichen Exercises* that I have developed. These exercises were actually designed for a horse in a bridle but they are also very, very good for horses that are fearful. The reason that they work so well on a fearful horse is because they make the horse conscious; they make him be present in the moment. As you hold his head, he has to concentrate and this allows him to give up his fear and he begins to relax.

These *Uberstreichen Exercises* (which are coming out on DVD) work very much like when we go to a masseur for a massage. After the massage, we get off the table and how do we feel? We feel as if all the problems we had when we came in have just melted away and don't exist anymore. That's exactly what the *Uberstreichen Exercises* do because the horse gives up the fear and struggle and just settles in to being present in the moment, right here right now with you. As you probably know, when you do this, it feels really, really good and the horse experiences that too.

Encouraging Horses to the Next Level

Recently we did some filming with wild horses at Return to Freedom, a non-profit wild horse sanctuary near Lompoc, California. I was there working with a horse that was very shy. We were doing this filming because I wanted to show a horse that was really afraid of humans, and this particular horse was definitely scared to death of people. I don't know what his history was but despite whatever had happened to him, I was able to get him comfortable enough to eat out of a bucket that I was holding. However he was still very frightened because he was grabbing a mouthful and then jumping back, almost knocking the bucket out of my hand.

As I said, he was just really very, very frightened and he was doing something else, too. When he was eating out of the bucket, he liked to hit the bottom of it with his teeth, as if he was trying to grab the food or bite at it rather than just eat it. When a horse does this, I will take the bucket away from him and then give back, so that he realizes that every time he bites the bottom of the bucket, it goes away. He learns that he has to be more gentle. He is doing this, of course, because he is scared. After I did this for a while, he became more comfortable, so then I wanted to get him to take it to the next level.

Now, we cannot just expect a horse just to take himself to the next level; we have to encourage him. So, the next thing I did was to touch the end of his nose with my hand before I allowed him to go in the bucket and eat. The reason a horse will let you do this is because when he is nursing as a baby, his nose touches the top of the mother's belly. So when you do this, not only are you bringing him forward to the next level but I believe you are actually hitting neural pathways in the horse's brain to make him feel nurtured. From there, you can really develop a close relationship. That is the sort of work I do with shy horses.

How to Tackle a Fearful and Aggressive Horse?

This article carries a question, which I think many of you might find interesting and valuable. It concerns an Arab mare that is alternately fearful and aggressive and is generally uneasy around other horses. Tami writes:

I have a lovely 17 year old Arab mare that I acquired as a green-broke 10 year old and have spent lots of time working with over the last 7 years. She is very bonded to me and when I moved from the East Coast and then up to Canada from San Diego a few years ago she came with me. She lived most of her life very happily on a farm where each horse stayed in an individual paddock and only socialized over fences.

My issue with my little girl is other horses. With me, away from other horses, she is perfect. She obeys happily, loves to 'groom' me and rests with her nose on my shoulder, just oozing happy vibes. However as soon as another horse enters the picture she goes into alternating aggressive and afraid modes, squealing and striking at the other horse and then cowering. In a mare herd she is always the bottom horse. We've tried her with all sorts of horses and she won't go past a sort of uneasily watchfulness. I've never seen her groom another horse or stand nose to tail peacefully swatting flies as the others do.

She is more confident when I'm riding, but on the ground she becomes unpredictable, once knocking the barn manager down (whom she loves) in a seemingly random moment of panic and another time running through a metal gate like she didn't even see it. It is worst when she is in season and she's gotten herself hurt on fences twice. She won't focus on her handler and fixates on the other horses. I have her at home now, with one other mare that is bossy but not mean. My mare is clearly wary of her but they will generally graze in peace during their turnout together. Is there anything I can do to help her overcome her fear at this point or do I just need to manage her environment the best I can to keep her in her own paddock? I hate to see her so unsettled (also makes her a hard keeper) and I'm afraid she will hurt herself or another horse in one of her fits.

My answer:

It is wonderful that you care about your horse so much. My suggestion is that you develop her ability to stay focused on you. Since she is used to being moved off her grazing spot this will be very easy to teach her to do. Your mare would be helped a lot my two of my *Waterhole Rituals™* - *Eye Contact* and *Leading from Behind*.

To start the *Eye Contact* ritual, put some hay in the center of the area where you will be working with your horse. Choose the hay that she would enjoy eating. Be careful that she is not too hungry because this could bring out the aggressive side of a horse. Many times, I use oat hay. With some horses, such as those who are picky eaters, I will use alfalfa.

Start this exercise when your horse has settled down to the idea of eating. When she is interested in eating, stand about fifteen feet in front of her head. Wait about four minutes and then take a step to the right and stand there for a moment or two. Cluck to get her to look at you and then go back to your original position if she looks at you. If she doesn't look, take another step to the right and cluck again. Keep this up by stepping around her, keeping the same fifteen-foot distance. Any time she looks at you, go back to standing in front of her, and let her eat for a while. That way she gets a quick reward.

If she never looks at you, keep taking steps around her until you are at her backend. Wait and then drive her from the hay. Remember, she should go easily because of the *Leading from Behind* and the *Taking Territory* rituals. The object is that your horse learns to keep her attention on you when you ask her to. Also, she learns that she can control you with a look and that is good for a horse that needs more self-confidence.

Leading from Behind will also be helpful in developing her coping skills and the ability to pay attention to you. The way to begin is to follow her around in the paddock when she stops. Wait a moment and then ask her to move. When she walks, follow her again and repeat. If she trots off to get away from you, walk slowly after her. When you reach her, pause with her a while and then ask her to move on and repeat. It might not make any sense but you should see a big difference in her behavior after 30 days of this kind of training. It is how horses train other horses to fit in. My book *Naked Liberty* is how all these kinds of training tips are used by horses in nature to bring about proper social behavior and a unified herd. As this is about shaping her character, one thing to keep in mind is that character can be shaped but you cannot change the basic nature of how she is. You will know more about her basic personality and who she is by this practice.

Managing Anxiety Separation of a Mare and her Foal

This question comes from Victoria, who is a regular contributor and has her own blog at www.victoriacummings.blogspot.com

I just took your quiz and the one question that I answered "no" to made me want to ask your advice. I have two Quarter Horses, a mare (who is 20 years old) and her daughter (who is 6 years old). They live together, without other horses - although prior to being in my backyard, I had them in a herd of 6 horses - and it has become difficult to separate one from the other. Mostly, it is Mama Silk who gets upset when her baby, Siete, is out of eyesight. Silk is very closely bonded to me, so it may partly be jealousy that I'm going away with the other horse. She gets so upset, calling and racing back and forth. What can I do to help her realize that we'll be back soon and that everything is okay?

I'm really enjoying your blog, and it's very generous of you to help. I read Naked Liberty about a year ago and it really opened my mind to new possibilities with my girls. It's great that you have started doing videos. I look forward to seeing the Waterhole Ritual™ DVD.

In reply:

Thank you first of all for your kind comments. Even though these feelings are very natural for a horse who does not want to be left alone, I have always been able to fix the problem you are having with a horse like Mama Silk. It will take some effort and time but is lots of fun if you enjoy tinkering with your horses.

When you and Siete leave the paddock do it at the time the horses are fed and then groom Siete near her mother on the opposite side of the fence. After a few minutes, lead her a short distance away and return her to her mother. Make sure that on the way you have some grain in a bucket at various spots along the path you are traveling so Siete is thinking that it is a good thing to leave her mother. Then bring her back to Mama Silk and let her mother settle down, repeat this many times.

If Siete or her mother is having a hard time with the process let her eat her food as far away from her mother as her mother will tolerate before venturing on short trips. Have two piles of food; one very close and another some distance away. Put both piles in a place so that both mother and baby can see each other. It will take about five days, maybe longer.

Any time the horses get nervous take Siete back to where she is not nervous and start in on another adventure. Take Siete to places she can graze for a short time, maybe a minute to start with, and then bring her back to her mother. Her mother should be absorbed in eating. If not, use Equine Senior to sweeten the pot and keep her daughter coming and going in short little trips each day.

Make sure that any extra food is removed when you leave. This way Mama Silk will understand that she missed an opportunity and next time she will have more desire to eat her treat food when it is presented to her.

Hope this is some help. Let me know how it goes and how you got the job done. Your biggest problem lies in that fact that you only have two horses. This will be a little harder to accomplish. The good news is that it can be fixed. I found that horses adjust to almost anything if they can expect what is happening as a daily routine.

FREQUENCY OF TRAINING

Routine Training can be Very Useful with Horses

This story is about a horse named, Serpico. Now, Serpico was an Arabian gelding that I purchased at auction and he was just an absolutely beautiful Arabian. He was 16 hands, liver chestnut, just gorgeous and we actually got him for very little money.

This didn't make sense because he was such a nice horse but after we got him home, we started to get calls saying, "How is Serpico?" and "Are you okay?" And I would say, "Ooh, he's doing wonderfully and is such a great horse." But we got more and more calls asking about Serpico, so I asked one of the callers why they were asking.

Well, we found out that on the auction floor the day before we bought him, Serpico had broken and run away from a fabulous trainer, whom no horse had ever intimated before. In fact, Serpico had broken his arm and attacked another horse, so he was considered a complete outlaw.

When I saw him in the auction, I knew nothing about the story, bought him and thought he was just wonderful. Serpico gave us no problems and the reason that he didn't was because we never asked him to do anything that he didn't want to do nor did he feel threatened.

When I found all this out, I started taking a real interest in getting to know Serpico very well. One of the things that I would do with him was to visit him at night, at maybe 2 am, just to see how he was. From those visits, I learned a couple of things. I learned to teach a horse to lie down and I learned it's good to visit and handle a difficult horse at night rather than during the daytime. For some reason, at that time of night, horses are very, very friendly and happy to see you. I have used that method to train horses from that time on, particularly aggressive horses, because it's just an absolutely fabulous way of taking a mean horse and making him sweet and tractable.

So when I used to go out at 2 am, I found that Serpico was always lying down. I used to take him a bowl of water mixed with a little wine and honey and I would put it under his little nose to drink.

This went on for a while and I realized I had an opportunity to teach this horse to lie down. So I started going out a little earlier, at maybe 1:30 am, and sure enough he had not laid down yet. I went to him with my bowl of water, wine and honey and he looked at me as if to say, "It must be time for my nightcap." I looked at him and said, "No, you can't have that wine until you lie down." and he did because that was our routine.

So you see how you can use little tricks like this, combined with routine, to help train your horse.

Working Horses on a Regular Basis....or not?

The lesson I would like to discuss today is how our horses behave when they have not been worked on a regular basis.

Normally, if we turn a horse out in a big field and just leave him for a week or maybe a month and then bring him back to ride, he will often be just wild. Most horses need to be worked on a daily basis, five days a week so that we can depend on them not to be too out of control. I find that interesting because horses we train with the *Waterhole Rituals* ™do not have that problem.

We can turn them loose for a week, a month or a year, bring them back, jump on them and we don't have to go through the process of getting them accustomed to being ridden again. The reason for this is because the training was done in a joyful way, and the connection with the horse is so beautiful that you do not have to take the edge off them because there isn't any edge. They have had their social behavior shaped so they know how to fit in with you, regardless of whether you've been away for a short time or even a long time.

What made me think about this is I went to see an Andalusian stallion called Panadero. I had not worked with Panadero in over three months and in fact, he had hardly been worked at all and had been housed in a stall. Now you would think that a horse that had been housed in a stall with no interaction with people would be out of control. Well, I worked with him and it was like he had been in training every single day. He was perfect.

When we stopped working together three months ago, he didn't really have the Spanish Walk mastered. He could maybe do 25 feet at liberty when I asked him. However, the day I worked him he was so excited to do the Spanish Walk again, he did it for 100 feet and would have kept going except he ran out of room in the arena. It was just so beautiful and everybody thought it was great.

So if you focus on *Waterhole Rituals™* and you are focused on developing manners and the quality of connection, when you next go visit your horse you will have a horse that is as perfect as Panadero was that day.

Horse Training Takes Time....or does it?

I just came back in today from training a horse by the name of Marchador. I was thinking about him after our session and I could not believe how far we have come together.

It has been so exciting working with him through the *Waterhole Rituals™*. Today, we were working on the last Ritual, which is *Go Trot and Come Up.* What you want here is that when you send your horse off, he runs away at top speed. Then you call him back, and he turns around and runs back as fast as he left. This is what I got today with Marchador. It was absolutely brilliant. He did it three times straight on his own. I did not ask for a fourth time. I was thrilled at where he is at this time in his life and the training he has done so far.

I'm not going to go into everything he does now but I do want to talk about how I started with him and how he used to be. When he came to me, he was very angry. He did not like people. He was in fact responsible for breaking both a woman's arms. He would attack any horse that came near him. When he came here and went out in the paddock, he would go to the far end of it and stand there and just be really mad, aggressive and fearful. So how I got him to the point that he is at today is an amazing testament to the power of the *Waterhole Rituals™*.

Given how he was back then, the first *Waterhole Ritual™* alone was so valuable. I spent probably three months with that horse not doing anything but sitting in his paddock and reading a book with him. What took place during that time was amazing, even the first time I did this with him. He realized pretty quickly that I didn't want anything from him, I was just out there for his company and he was free to do exactly what he wanted. I was sitting in a chair and when he came up to me and started interacting. He was like a sweet, gracious child. He started to become a different horse, and I just let that relationship build for the first three months.

To show how powerful this process is, when you look at him today, you would say that he has been in training for a couple of years. Would you be surprised to hear then, that we have only been working together for a total of six months? So that three months of sitting in the chair and letting him interact with me and me not interact with him was time totally well spent as he got to have his relationship the way he wanted it. And I got to find out what a very kind and lovely horse he is.

So, my question to you is do you spend enough time with your horse? When was the last time you just hung out together? If you want to reward an animal, the best you can reward him is with companionship and so that is what I recommend you do with your horse.

MAKING TRAINING FUN

How to Deal With Boredom in Horses

This is from a lady called Jan, who wrote:

I have an off-track thoroughbred (OTTB) who is extremely intelligent and over-reactive, has had many bad habits from racing and is easily bored. He also resents being told what to do so I really work to find what he likes to do best. He has had foot problems for the past three years but is now sound. We have been through a lot together and he really trusts me but he does not always listen. I still have trouble keeping his attention all the time. And any time he does not want to do something that he thinks is boring, he throws a huge fit!

He was obviously forced to do things and beaten before I bought him. He hates having whips pointed at him but I can stroke him with a TTEAM wand. He is a wonderful, sweet horse with a big heart and is also a comedian. I am looking for ways to work with him that will be acceptable to him given his background. He is adverse to force and coercion. He has made great progress but I still have trouble. How can your techniques help this horse?

Here's my reply:

It sounds to me you have a caring nature and you are an experienced horsewoman. In response to your question, my answer is Yes!

My Method would be most valuable to you and your horse, and the problems you are having with your horse are exactly the issues it is designed to fix - like trust, motivation, force, wellness and nature.

I want to point out that he does not need to be fixed. I do not believe his fitful behavior needs to be fixed. I would calm him down when he throws a fit and ask him to do something he would enjoy doing and develop a program that you know he would respond well to and that would not bore him. I have trained hundreds of horses with my Method and I have never found a horse that the Method bored. Boredom is a sign he is being asked to do something he does not want to do. I only work with a horse when he is willing to work. I give him a reason to want to work.

Before I start any training I build attitude focus, respect and a desire to learn and perform. I first shape the horse's character to fit in harmony with me before I expect any performance out of him. I must build a willing attitude in the horse to want to pay attention and have a desire to learn new behaviors. But even before that I must build a bond strong enough that the horse would trust me as much as he would trust his own Mom. He would not be afraid of me with a whip in my hand. Your horse still does not trust you enough because he is still afraid of a whip and he also does not approve of your program from your description of his boredom.

Your horse will be happy to hear that working the way I do there is no force or coercion. My Method works with the desire and instincts of the horse only. I work a horse at liberty around food that is on the ground that he would like to have and if he wants the food he must listen to me. One of my first lessons I offer a horse is that he can eat all the hay he wants if he's keeping an eye on me. This builds a habit in staying focused. Horses love this game and take to it right way. The program is designed to be enjoyable to the horse and his owner. He gets many puzzles to solve and enjoys solving them. He leads the way to his own development through what he responds to.

I shape his character to have a work ethic, and if your horse is a clown he naturally has an ability for a work ethic; he just needs my program to get him started off on the right foot.

The reason my Method is the Foundation for all Equestrians Pursuits is that once you develop a working partnership with it, everything you do with your horse will be received with a desire to learn. My program is not interested in performance it is interested in connection, communication and partnership building. With my Method you will develop a superior communication system that is magical. Once the trust issues are handled he will not over-react. The over-reaction is only your horse's desire to be understood. I do not think a horse should have to fit into a program. I think a program should fit the horse and his specific personality.

Horse Training Game

When you are training your horse, you shouldn't be too interested in his performance. Instead of developing the bond to be able to train your horse, you should use the training to deepen the bond you have with him.

The horse will direct your leadership and you should offer the program. This kind of leadership is comforting and nurturing to a horse. When a horse does not live in a harmonious herd environment, he needs us to provide socialization and leadership for his emotional well-being.

In developing a method for horses, we need to allow the horse the ability to figure out how to fit in and work within our system without him feeling pressured. Not approaching him and waiting for him to come to us will develop his desire to learn how to fit in with us. Allowing a horse to become interested builds his self esteem and increases his ability to partner up with us from a willing heart.

Here's the game I came up with, hope you like it.

Start your horse out at liberty in an arena or large round pen. This exercise takes two or three people and in fact it works with as many as you like. Sit in chairs about 20 feet apart and have some carrots with you under your chair. When your horse goes up to a person, they give him one carrot and no more. If the horse becomes a nuisance, begging for another carrot, shoo him away like a kindly mare would shoo a foal way when she does not want him to nurse. The horse will eventually leave and go to someone else and when he does, this person gives him one carrot and no more. Keep repeating one carrot per visit, per person. Do not try to guide him to go see someone else, just shoo him away. He can go where he likes. All we want to do is to challenge him to figure out how to work the system. If three people are playing this game and the horse just goes between two people that is alright because we are just teaching him that one carrot is all that he gets per visit and he learns that being driven away is a prelude to another carrot. He learns that to be driven away has a great reward and meaning. You want him to figure this out on his own.

Your role is to say no more carrots and leave me alone with any miming gestures, voice and body language that work. After he learns this, you will increase the difficulty for him by choosing the person that will offer him the next carrot. If he is begging from a person that is not chosen, that person will point to the person that is chosen and say to the horse go to and say the person's name. This way the horse will learn names. The person that the horse is being sent to will call the horse as well. Both people encourage the horse to go to the person of choice. Continue this exercise. Once the horse has this down-pat, place your chairs far apart and encourage the horse to trot and walk to the person who has the carrot, then eventually ask the horse to canter from person to person as directed. You can make your own variation as you wish to advance the horse's schooling. The horse will show great enthusiasm for the freedom he experiences and the direction he receives and being the center of attention like a child.

Imagine what it might feel like if the roles were reversed. We are minding our own business when we come across a horse. We walk up to get a closer look and in our closeness, we receive from the horse a thousand dollar bill. We find that every horse we encounter will give up money and as the relationship grows, they direct us to were the next honey (or should that be money) pot is.

Good luck and remember if you have problems doing this lesson, stop the exercise. I do not want horses and humans frustrated. I am sure I will have other exercises later on that may work better for you and your horse.

Mr Post and the Little Foal

I like to tie my horses to a post because I think it is a fabulous way to develop a more dependable horse. Before I tie a horse, I teach the horse to stand still at liberty on command using the *Waterhole Rituals™*. If it is a foal, I make certain that foal would be happy being separated from its mother and vice versa. From being tied, a horse learns that when I leave him he is responsible for standing still and not fussing.

At the beginning of the training, I tie him with a knot that I can pull loose immediately should he suggest he would pull back. The theory is that in early training if a horse never experiences pulling back, he will not choose it as an option later on when he is fully trained.

So, let's say I have a baby foal that has a foundation with the *Waterhole Rituals™* and this baby foal watches his mother regularly being tied to a post and he sees how much she enjoys it and how happy she is. He thinks to himself, "Gee, I never get tied to that post".

So, one day, you bring that little foal and you say "Today's the day! Today we're going to tie you to Mr. Post." And the foal says, "Boy, you been bringing everyone else and tying them to the post and I've never been to the post before. I'm sure glad I get to investigate Mr. Post today".

You say "Yes" and you tie him up, "Now, there you are with Mr. Post". And he says "Mmm, very interesting post". "And I'm just going to sit right here in this chair and keep you company. Oh, and by the way, here's a carrot. Well, isn't this fun here with Mr. Post? Well, I'm just going to read my book here for a while. OK, we've been here three minutes, that's enough, let's untie you."

And the foal says "Boy, I can't wait to go to Mr. Post again, that was so much fun".

So the next day you bring that little foal up again and tie him to Mr. Post and he says "Oh here I am with Mr. Post again!" Now, it's not a post, it's a tree, a beautiful tree and the foal says "Oh I just love being here under this post with all its leaves and shade".

"Yes" I say, "You don't have to worry about a thing, I'm right here. Oh and by the way, here's your carrot."

So, as the days go by, you only have to hand him a carrot once in a while and the time between carrots gets longer and longer.

So pretty soon, I can say "Oh Honey, guess what? I've run out of carrot. You stay right here and I'll be right back" and I go and he's left there all by himself. And he's saying, "I wonder where she went?"

I'm gone a little while and then I come back, "Well here I am! I went to get some carrots for you. Good boy, here's your carrot".

And the foal says "Well, thank goodness, you went to get those carrots!"

Next time I go away a little longer and he says to himself, "I know where she's going! She's going to get those carrots".

So I go about my business, do the things I have to do and the next thing you know, 30 minutes have gone by.

Now that foal has a system of understanding that that's what we do. He says "I can stand here like my mother, you just watch me. I can stand here right by this post because I love standing here! See everybody, I'm standing by the post and you don't get to stand by the post. But I do and carrots are going to come".

The next thing you know, an hour has gone by and I come back and I say "You're right, Honey, here are those carrots, you're so lucky."

So one day somebody brings in a horse trailer. Now the little foal has never been in a trailer before but he's had lots of experience with Mr. Post and also, he's seen everybody else get in the horse trailer and eat.

And that foal says "When's it going to be my time to get in the trailer?"

So I say "Today is your turn to get in the trailer".

You know what that foal does?

He says "Get out of my way, I want to get in that trailer!" and in he goes. He stands there and says "This is much better than being with Mr. Post, you know., Look at all the treats in this trailer". And I let that baby eat those treats and just before he finishes them, I bring him out of the trailer and he says, "Wait a minute, I haven't finished those treats!"

"Oh, that's OK, Honey, we'll get them next time" I say.

And he's feeling really sad, he says "Gee, she took me out of that trailer and I didn't get to finish those treats". So by the next time that trailer comes round, he just can't wait to get into it.

So there you have it, pretty simple, huh? Well, yes and no. I surely haven't given you all the answers on how to accomplish the task of teaching a horse to be tied and after all, horses are individuals so some will be easy and others will require a bit more work. The rule of thumb, though, is that if there is any objection or concern, I do not tie. Maybe we just eat the carrot at the post and then return home.

If a foal becomes upset at any point on his trip to the post, stop and give him time to get comfortable. When he is, give him carrots and take him home. The main point is to let the foal's attitude and how he is feeling about what is going on guide your decisions.

The purpose of this tale is to empower you to find your own way to train a horse to be tied up by showing you the method I use and how careful I am to keep a horse interested and enthusiastic about learning new behaviors. So I hope you find that useful.

RIDING

How to Create a Bond before you Ride

Here are some tips on how to connect with your horse on a daily basis so that you can warm up the working bond between you before you ride.

1. Before you get to the barn, remember to clear you mind and make a mental outline of all the things you are going to do with your horse. Be prepared, however, to change course depending on how the connection with your horse goes and how he is feeling. Be in a good mood and happy to see your horse. Remember to give him your full attention as a horse finds it hard to follow your lead without your full attention. Try to see him around the same time each day so he looks forward to your arrival.

2. Remember to keep your eye on everything in your immediate environment that might influence your horse in some way so you can handle any changing situation appropriately.

3. When you get to your horse, spend some time with him in the moment and don't feed him treats until you know your horse is enjoying your company and you have his full attention. This way you are not just a serving wench or a vending machine. This is where I might use the *Eye Contact* Rituals. With my horses, I offer treats some days and others not, but most often I treat. I decide when I offer the treat by the attitude of my horse. If he is not bonding with me because he is looking around for treats that day, I hold them off for a more appropriate time. It usually takes only a few minutes to become connected without a treat.

4. I do not ride any more but when I used to ride, I would play through the *Waterhole Rituals™* building the connection before I would ride. This allows the bond to grow and flourish and to give the horse activities that he misses out on from not living in a community of horses. It gives a horse more life experiences and a sense of self. I check out if my horse is too shy or too self serving or not focused or too alive or not awake and then I make the adjustments while we are not serious and in a playful

state. Working on a relationship with a horse gives a horse a full sense of self worth while warming up our team-working skills together, especially when done around manners and food with games such as "You can eat here this time."

5. When I start my ride, I check out how my horse is responding to my aids. How responsive is he to the halt and go buttons and turning aids. Is he listening? How are his transitions? I then work on any adjustments before I ask for any performance. I spend a segment of time riding to warm the horse up in order to create relaxation and forward movements like a meditation. Again, this is an example of how to use a routine to build a connection.

6. When I ask a horse to walk or trot, I first find out the speed he wants to travel and when I determine that, I then ask him to go faster if his trot is on the slow side. If it is faster, I ask him to slow down. If it is just right, I still must ask for a change in speed. This way my horse will pay more attention to his job and have a better carriage to his gaits by bringing up his back to accommodate the change of pace. The change of pace will also help to develop more suspension in the stride.

7. When you have finished riding, take your horse out on a lead and let him graze or feed him in his paddock and read a book or journal to just spend time with your horse.

Warm Up Rituals for your Horse

Isaac Hayes, a well-known musician said, "you cannot bake bread in a cold oven". I think this is an appropriate analogy of how important it is to warm up a horse so as to have the best attitude and working bond possible each day before you ride.

It is therefore a good idea to warm a horse up every day to create an environment for the relationship to grow so the horse can get a feel for wanting to be ridden each day. You could take him out to graze and work with him on table manners or groom him while he is grazing and work on cooperation at the same time.

It is very important for a horse's emotional well-being to have some time with you in relationship before riding him. Sharing interactions with your horse before you ride is most important.

The segments of connection we need to focus on are the initial daily greeting. Then after the initial bond has been reunited, you can focus on adjusting your leadership and partnership connection with your horse. Then practice warming up the team-working connection. This is essential to prepare a horse properly.

All good horsemen do this but they don't speak about it enough and might not even notice they are doing just that. Part of this is due to their ability to read a horse when they approach him. It may not look like they are paying attention to these connections but if they find a lack of connection on greeting their horse, they restore the relationship before they get on.

We must always remember that a horse is not a lawn mower or a 4-wheel drive vehicle kept in the garage. We shouldn't take him for granted. He is a living being as we are, and he is always growing and can change his attitude about his performance and the connection he shares with you. That is why we need to take the time each day to re-establish the connection even if the horse seems ready to go.

Riding is all About Connecting with the Horse

I am going to tell you story about my first job outside of my own business and ranch where I grew up in Indio, California. The job was in La Jolla, California, at a large riding academy and I looked at all these beautiful riders there. They were riding hunters and jumpers and I thought they looked better than I did on a horse. And so I said, "I don't know why you would hire me train these people because they seem to be riding better than I do". The academy people said, "No, no, no, no, you watch them". So I watched them and I saw that when a horse refused to take a fence and ran out on the left that the person was thrown off the horse. I saw that even when they were just cantering around that if a horse just moved the wrong way, off went the rider because they did not have any balance.

They had not become connected to their horses and I realized that connection can't happen in lessons. It has to come from the connection that you have on a horse. The connection you have when you are not under instruction. So when I teach people how to ride, what I do is I pay more attention to how the person feels while they are on the horse. How do they feel on this horse? If I tell them to put their heels down when they are not really connected to their horse, it's a waste of time and plus it makes them a brittle rider. If you want to learn how to ride correctly on a horse, what you want is someone to tell you when to do things at the time that's most going to help you.

I rode in the desert for years on horses that I trusted and felt balanced upon and I became such a part of the horse. Someone saw me riding when I was about 14 and they said, "We want you to show our horse" and I said, "Well, I don't know too much about riding a western horse" and they said, "Well, it doesn't make any difference, you just come on down anyway and we want you to show this mare in western pleasure and trail horse classes".

So I went down and they showed me how my heels should be, how my knees should be, how my back should be, how my hands should be and how everything should be. It turned out I was the high point of the show because I felt connected with my horse and I knew how to get my horse to feel connected to me and that is the secret. The secret is that you feel connected and he feels connected to you. Then when you are told to put your heels down or to do this or to do that, you are empowered in a way that does not make you a brittle or unbalanced rider.

Loss of Performance when Riding

I deal with a loss of performance under saddle using the activities surrounding the *Waterhole Rituals™* as we are doing fun stuff together at liberty. Like the game, *"Look at me and eat all you want, or come with me and I will take you to the food."* I gain co-operation and respect over food issues rather than asking a horse to perform a self-serving act under saddle. The *Waterhole Rituals™* prepares the horse to perform under saddle perfectly by priming him to be focused, willing, connected and having the right energy to perform at its best under saddle.

You will approach your horse much differently at liberty than when you are working with a horse under saddle because under saddle you are focused on the performance rather that the teamwork and quality of connection. At liberty, you will take the time and deal directly with issues of why the horse is not performing well under saddle with a kinder attitude. In this state of mind, you can put all of your attention on developing the connection instead of trying to get a horse to perform when the connection is not quite right.

I never train a horse through resistance at the time he becomes resistant. I stop working with the horse when I hit resistance, put him back at liberty, and develop a better connection. I do not want anyone to address a horse when there is resistance because by pushing the performance to get control over your horse can cause a horse to not like his performance. This is not fun for the horse and an unskilled person will most likely lose the battle anyway.

The *Waterhole Rituals™* handles the partnership and relationship issues in a simple fashion. This way, you never pressure the horse in his performance. If a problem occurs on the horse's back, you settle the problem with the rituals on the ground when the horse is in a better frame of mind. In this way, the horse will not develop a bad attitude about being ridden

My book *Naked Liberty* is meant to help people learn the true nature of horses and if you have not read my book, I would suggest that you order it. Being a confident leader comes from having the right point of view to be able to lead without force. There is a time to lead, a time to pause, a time to court the relationship and a time to hold a horse responsible for his conduct.

Tips for Amateur Trail Riders

It is often more beneficial to grain your horse out on the trail than at home to help barn-sour horses. If the horse tries to go home faster, turn him around after an eighth of a mile and ride him back to the spot you grained him and give him some more grain. You can repeat this several times on a daily ride. This could fix your horse from wanting to get home in a hurry. It is so much fun watching the horse change his mind and reconsider his options.

Another tip is to always walk your horse home. Do not trot and canter. Many beginning trail riders enjoy playing 'pony express rider' on their ride home but allowing your horse to run home builds up bad habits in the horse as well as builds bad habits in yourself.

You want your horse to be cooled down before you get him home so his muscles are kept in condition. On your way back, work on halting and stand for five minutes two or three times so your horse gets accustomed to the idea that going home is a quiet relaxed trip. You could also ride half way home, then turn around and go somewhere else. This is excellent for management on a green trail horse as it doesn't allow a horse to get stuck in a routine that does not work in your favor.

You can train horses easily through the routines you develop for them but it can also work against you too. Dressage riders can have the same problems with their horses. When a horse learns a routine, many times they will pay more attention to performing their routine and not listen to your direction.

Letting Other People Ride Your Horse

I have spoken before about preparation before you ride but I was recently asked a question about letting other people ride your horse and wanted to make sure I had explained it clearly.

Do not let anyone ride your horse unless you believe they have the skill to get along with him or can put more training on him for you. Horses can be offended and lose their training by having a stranger on their backs. Most people have few or no skills in making a connection with a strange horse for the first time. On the other hand, I have watched people get on horses and need no time at all to find out how a horse needs to be ridden.

It takes some effort to learn how to ride not too aggressively and not too passively. To learn how much to correct a horse, when to leave him alone, when to be precise and when to allow him to lead. You can develop your skill and help the connection between you through your preparation and daily warm-ups.

Horse Riding with Spurs

Today's story concerns the use of spurs. I was prompted to write it as I've just finished doing an article where I was speaking about the use of whips and spurs in training. It reminded me of the first time that I discovered that there was such thing as a spur. I think I must have been about ten years old when I saw somebody riding with spurs and I didn't know what they were. So I asked my father, "What are on those on the boots?"

"Well, those are spurs."

"What do you use them for?" I asked.

My father said, "They're decoration."

"Oh!" I said, "They're very pretty."

"Yes, they are also used to show off."

"What do you mean, show off?"

"Well, if somebody wears spurs, it's a sign that they are a great horseman. So people that are not so good with horses do not ride with spurs and people who are great horsemen ride with spurs" he replied.

"Why would that be so?" I asked.

"Well Carolyn, try riding bareback in spurs and see how long you can stay on your horse." He went on to explain that if your leg is in the right place, you will not prick the horse with the spur, meaning that you can ride very well and I actually thought that was what spurs were for. So, I got myself spurs and I showed in gymkhana classes bareback doing weaving patterns at top speed, riding in spurs and showing off. I had no idea they were ever used as a training aid.

I just thought it was a cute story and a wonderful thing to tell anybody who really wants to develop a better seat. So, my suggestion is to use spurs to develop a better seat and not to use them to prick the horse. What do you think?

Planning on Starting Horse Riding and Taking Lessons

I often get asked about starting horse riding and so I thought I would give you some tips for those of you in that position and also for those who think they are having some 'control' issues.

For your first horse experience, choose a horse that you can trust and is very willing to take care of you. By developing confidence with a horse that you can trust, you will be more effective later on as your skills naturally evolve. If your lessons are not fun, seek another teacher and if the horse causes you fear and anxiety, choose a different horse.

Your yardstick for making the right decision with horses should be on how much fun you and your horse are having together. When you choose a horse, choose a size of horse that fits your frame and whose gaits are enjoyable and comfortable to ride.

It is very important that in the beginning, you have a horse that doesn't need to be corrected for not doing what you want him to do for you. So, choose a well-trained willing horse that is known as a babysitter.

If you have a horse that is not dependable and needs to be kept in line, your focus turns to correction rather than leading and the more you are into correction the more unable you are to lead. Your first focus must be on leadership and that is all you should have to focus on as it takes time to direct a horse properly.

The first thing to acquire before you get into control issues is to allow your body to lead the rhythm of the horse and how to lead through the rhythm rather than correction. Until you stop focusing on correction, it is very hard to pay attention to the timing of your aid for direction. Correction is too much work at this time since you do not have the skill. Usually, what you will create is more and more resistance and a bigger problem in trying to correct your horse and you will lose your leadership.

Horses ridden improperly can lose their training. A beginner does not know how to communicate through their body and the horse will begin to wander. A beginner just sits on a horse like a load of laundry and allows the horse to carry them rather than to stay one step ahead of the horse and choose a direction while matching the rhythm of the horse. If you stay focused on your timing, the control of the horse's speed and where you are going, that is quite enough to think about.

Try this lesson:

When you are on the trail, look at where you are going and feel your horse's body rhythm as you look at the point ahead and then, practice matching his rhythm at the same time your eyes are focused on where you are going. Then try to slow down your rhythm or speed it up and you will notice he will begin to respond to your rhythm.

The control is gained by asking for a little more or less speed, halt and pause or change of direction as a way to keep the harmony, unity and focus of your horse. The horse needs to be inspired from the connection he feels from you sitting while in focus and attention. Your attention and focus controls a horses' behavior and this takes practice.

First you need to learn what a true connection with a horse is before you can lead a horse appropriately. Ride under someone's guidance that is nurturing to people and horses and knows how to develop a beginner student.

Webster: Not Everyone Should Ride a Horse

Today I want to tell you a story about one man and his horse. This story sort of suggests that not everyone should ride a horse. Certain people can certainly ride with no problems but Webster was not one of them and I think you'll understand why when I tell you his story.

Well, Webster had two horses, one was a pony and other was a nice older horse. He'd had lots of failures with riding the pony and this one time was thrown off onto the pavement and hurt himself quite badly. In fact, every time he seemed to get on a horse, he seemed to get thrown off. So, we decided that what he needed to do was ride the older horse so nothing would happen to him because that mare never did anything wrong, just never.

So Webster started riding this old mare and it was fine although he was still quite nervous. Anyway, the third time he rode the mare, he decided he wanted to go by himself because he felt that it was the crowd that had caused him to get hurled off previously. He took Sherry out and he was gone for a long time. In fact, he did not come back until very late and we were quite afraid. What had happened to Webster?

Around evening time, we eventually saw Webster coming back on Sherry and sure enough, he was still on the mare. But as he has got closer, we could see that he didn't look very good, in fact he was a bit of a battered, bloody mess. We assumed he must have been thrown off again. "What happened?" we asked him and you'll never believe what he said.

He had ridden Sherry out into the Water District in Ross, California and while he was coming home, a stallion who was at liberty on the hill had spied them. This stallion had rushed down because he smelled Sherry was in heat and he had bred that mare all the way home and poor Webster could not get off!

And that's what happened to Webster and it's just one of the funniest stories I've heard in all my life. Hope you enjoyed it!

CHAPTER SIX
CHALLENGING CONVENTIONAL WISDOM

WHERE TO TRAIN YOUR HORSE

Selecting an Area to Train Your Horse In

What I would like to talk to you about is how to use an area to develop a willing attitude in a horse.

The reason that you need to think about the area is that horses are very territorial. Also, if they have experienced a predator in a certain area, when they return there they are insecure. We can use this to work for us by taking our horse to the arena where we are going to be doing the training; we can get him to the fall in love with the area by feeding him his favorite food there and then taking him home again. So when he comes back to the arena, the horse says, "Boy, I just love being in this arena" and that's how I use territory in relationship to training a horse.

I use territory to train in another way. If I am training a horse to do a new thing, I will always take him to the same spot. That way, he understands that any time that he comes to that spot he knows that he is going to learn something new. So, now I get him to enjoy that spot by taking him there, giving him some food and letting him stay there until he becomes perfectly relaxed. I do that a few times so that he knows that this is the spot where bliss is found and then I train him with the new behavior. Let's say that I am working at liberty, doing tricks. I will take my horse to the spot and ask him to do a complicated trick. By then he knows that this spot is where I will always ask him to do something complicated. Now, if I walk him up to the spot and he is at liberty and he looks at me and says, "I'm not going to that spot because that's just too complicated to me," it is a heads up to me that I need to come up with something that is a little easier, a little more enjoyable to the horse. But if the horse steps up on that spot with a smile on his face, then I know that I can ask him for anything that I want and he is going to make a true effort.

You may ask how you get willing participation from your horse whenever you want it rather than just on one spot. Well, say you are training your horse to do simple things like stop. Just know that when you have trained him to stop on one spot and then you ask him to stop someplace else in the arena, you might have to school him on that new spot as well because of this territorial nature that horses have. Little by little though, as you work with your horse, you can get him to stop at this place and that place and then another place until finally he will stop at any place.

As you will see, all this takes time and patience, but then all good things do and are so worth it in the end, don't you think? Actually though, the truth is, time spent like this developing the bond and understanding between the two of you will considerably decrease the time you need to spend in the future with whatever further training you do together.

Limitations of Round Pens in Creating Magnetic Leadership

The old system of round penning has been glossed over by fancy words. I remember when I was a child, I was told that a round pen was used for breaking a horse's spirit. Then it was shortened to "breaking a horse," and today it is said to be a way to start a horse that would "develop a bond."

Round pens and ropes are wonderful tools but they are often misused. Ropes are often used to jerk a horse into submission. Round pens are too often used as a tool to gain a horse's trust by the horse running themselves ragged into submission. The round pen was designed so that the human can always influence the horse and the horse can never escape his handler's influence. In my view this is too much pressure on a horse to start forming a proper relationship with him. The bond gained from the inability to escape is created from a dominant leadership pursuit. I clearly would not use one to start a relationship with a horse. It isn't easy on a horse nor is it natural.

The natural way a horse develops a bond with the lead horse is to bond with the lead horse first first before he will follow his lead. The lead horse waits till the bond is in place. I call that kind of leadership magnetic leadership. The leader is chosen rather than made. A horse in the wild will gravitate to a lead horse he feels will protect him. Horses try to stay away from a horse that is too dominant. A round pen establishes a bond and leadership by a dominant leadership approach, just what a horse would naturally like to avoid.

This takes the instincts out of a horse, decreases his ability to learn and perform from his lack of interest, his attitude of submission and resigned complacency. Not wanting to create this response, I am careful that the horse never perceives me as a predator that he cannot escape from or as another aggressive horse.

Looking at the dynamics of leadership with horses requires clarifying the meaning of a true bond. The bond that occurs with a hostage and its kidnapper is not the bond I want to establish with a horse. I do not want a horse to feel he is a captured slave as the round pen creates. I have even wondered how people can learn leadership skills with humans by horsemanship methods that force a horse to bond with him by successfully proving to the horse that there is no escape. Leadership communication is knowing about when to communicate with someone in the moment to get a positive result, not from creating submission by force. It is critical to distinguish the difference between a compliant performance and a passionate performance. If a horse is pursued and forced to accept training the performance is based on survival and will be reflected with a loss of enthusiasm. If the performance is based on the horse choosing the performance there will be more enthusiasm and passion in the performance.

The way I work with a horse is if I know I will not get a positive response I do not try to communicate with him. I work with him in the 'yes' factor and build the horse to wanting to say 'yes' all the time, rather than ferreting out the resistance and eradicating it. My focus on the experience of training is to be interesting and enjoyable to the horse. I also make sure I build his self esteem and gain leadership through exhibiting to him that I am a leader that will take care of his needs as a way to create an enjoyable trustworthy saddle horse.

The Place for the Round Pen in Training

I want to make it clear that I am not condemning the use of round pens entirely. They certainly do have their place in training and I use them extremely regularly. What I am saying is that in my personal opinion, they are not the place to start building the bond with a horse, which I believe is absolutely essential to any sort of shared performance. So let me talk a little about bonding.

Bonding with horses has been thrown around a lot especially in terms of so-called natural horsemanship. Many of the leaders in natural horsemanship have been primarily men teaching women how to develop a bond with a horse. Working a horse with dominant leadership rather than magnetic leadership to establish a bond is very natural to alpha male behavior. What is natural to a human in their approach to horses is not natural to a horse for the bonding aspect.

Men teach horses that they have no way to escape their influence, and they want to set a horse straight. Eventually the horse will have to face the music and dance whether it wants to or not. This concept is hard for many women to grasp. Some women want to bribe their horse by offering them a carrot as a way to gain respect and leadership. Neither the carrot nor the dominant leadership approach establishes a true bond with a horse.

However, interacting with horses in the same manner that other horses do, does begin to develop a bond that lasts. Both leadership styles are beneficial and need to be blended. Women are on the right track to forming a bond from the carrot approach but need some nurturing guidance on setting boundaries. Many times they lose the respect of their horse by not knowing how to set boundaries and not understanding that leadership is a full time job that they are responsible for. Alpha male behavior should be put aside too and replaced by a magnetic influence to bring out the natural willingness of a horse, the way a woman likes to be courted.

All horses want to follow a leader, but when there isn't any leadership to follow, they think it is their job to lead. To gain a perfect partnership with a horse, it is important to connect with a horse through interactions that build a bond of trust that the horse respects. Developing this natural bond with your horse is essential before you start any program from riding, training, competition, or working in a round pen.

To clarify how to build a true bond with a horse one needs to step into the horse's world and follow their rules. Begin by using rituals that horses would use to gain a bond with each other rather than putting a horse in a false environment and taking their instinct of the flight for survival away from them. Working with horses is a marriage of true affection and respect. Before a horse is started with any training, including round pen training, he needs to feel a close friendship, trust and respect with a human and have no reason to want to escape the relationship he is sharing. Stepping into the horse's world and allowing the horse to shape our leadership, triggers the horse to follow our leadership naturally.

THE USE OF TREATS IN TRAINING

When to Give Your Horse Small Treats

In this article I would like to talk a little more about treats as it is an area that seems to cause many people a lot of confusion. When people are having difficulties with using treats, it is always because they haven't put the right foundations in place.

Treats work for me because I set a strong bond without treats first, and then I develop respect with a horse using treats. In formative training, I do not carry treats on me because it helps to keep the horse's attention on my direction instead of begging. In short, a horse will then perform what I ask without wanting a treat when I don't carry them with me. A horse will learn respect quickly if you put food on the ground; explain to him that the food is not his and that he needs to look for your direction to be told when he is allowed to eat and when he isn't, just like a nursing foal. By not having the treats on me, I notice the horse thinking more about his performance and trying to figure out what it is that I am asking him to accomplish and he loses interest in the treats very quickly.

Another way to use treats is with the *Taking Territory Ritual*, when you find your horse is running off too fast as if scared. What might slow him down is to put food all around and ask him to move a few steps, and then you walk away. Wait a few moments till your horse is comfortable, and then repeat but with the request to move further forward. You could stand behind him whilst he eats until he is comfortable. I only ask a horse to walk forward when he has stopped on a spot for a second or two and then I ask him to move forward maybe only one or two steps and then I wait and ask him again. It is fine to do just about anything at liberty, as long as you are not using the fence to trap the horse and he always has the ability to say 'no' to what you are asking him to do.

Offering Treats to Create a Magical Connection

I find that treats are an enjoyable way to socialize a horse to have a reliable character and willing attitude in his performances. Offering treats to horses may be the surprise answer to creating a magical connection with them!

Most trainers are against offering a horse treats for many good reasons. The most common is that a horse can become rude and spoiled, more interested in the treat than in the connection and the performance.

Often, the negative result of treats is created when people use them in training before the horse has been socialized to be polite and respectful with his human handler around food. Before I begin any training, I teach my horse that there are rules to be followed, just like the rules found in the natural herd. But if the treats ever do become a problem, I don't use them.

One of the first rules a horse learns from his mother is when he can nurse and when he cannot. Throughout their life, horses are shaping each other's behavior to a fine art of polite sharing of space and food. Most social politeness is generated around grazing. Since it works between horses, I have found that it works for me as well.

Due to his nature, the horse can perceive you giving treats by hand in two different ways. He can either perceive the treat as a gift from you, or he can perceive the treat as something he's taking from you against your will, even though you willingly handed him the treat. In the second case, given his pecking order nature, you lose his respect and thus the right to lead him. I believe that this is the reason it is commonly thought that giving treats to horses is not a good practice.

If you control a horse's behavior at the time you give him the treat from your hand, he can understand that the treat is a gift from you. When the treat is received as a gift, the horse is grateful and respectful and will exhibit polite behavior when he is in your charge.

With my approach, horses become more interested in connection with me and in our performance, rather than in the treat.

How to begin the socialization around the food treats is one of my first lessons for developing a meaningful friendship built on respect.

Try this yourself:

1. Start in his paddock at liberty with no tack when your horse feels relaxed. Place your treats on the opposite side of the fence out of reach. I have found that keeping the treats with me causes the horse to focus its attention on begging. I use carrots to treat, because they are safer than grain.
2. When your horse comes up to you, pet him.
3. After a short while of hanging out with your horse, ask him to leave. When he does leave and doesn't try to return, bring him a carrot.
4. Go back to the place by the fence where you have the carrots and wait. When he returns, pet him and then repeat the process.
5. When your horse seems to understand the routine, hold the carrot and wait for him to return. When he is approaching, ask him to stop with your voice. Step towards him as if you are going to drive him away from the area, like you have done before. If he halts, give him a carrot. If he does not halt, put the carrot back on the other side of the fence and go back to the beginning and start over. In a very short while, the horse should learn that the carrot is a gift you offering him rather than something he is taking away from you.

6. Your horse should eat the carrot slowly and gently and should also stop eating the carrot from your hand any time you tell him to wait. If he is not always gentle, start over from the beginning.
7. Once your horse understands that the carrot is a gift and you see an overall change in his attitude and behavior about treats, you can start using the carrots as a training aid. You could also return to this exercise any time your horse loses willingness, patience, politeness or respect.

Clicker Training and Treats

Someone asked me recently about clicker training and what I thought of it. Well, the fact of the matter is, I do not use clicker training.

I am not concerned about tricks and performance as much as I am about preparing a horse to accept training. Equally important to me are relationship bonding and connection with my horse. My focus is to shape a horse's character to be interested in learning and performing.

I like all forms of training if the horse learns though his natural instinct and the trainer makes every effort to develop a horse's interest and desire to learn and perform. It is important that the training be enjoyable to the horse. My Method is designed to prepare a horse for all training methods.

The same person then went on to ask me about treats and whether you should use them. The simple answer is if treats work, it is good to use them and if they don't work, it's not!

You see, a horse can work well with them one day and not the next day. So therefore, treats should be monitored. I find the biggest problem is that most people do not know how to prepare a horse to work well using treats. In my DVD *"Panadero's Journey"*, I share more specific information about handling food and treats whilst training and the proper way a horse should regard being fed.

Also, if you use treats in your training and then you find the horse cannot perform without them, you've just discovered that you didn't train your horse properly with regard to treats. There is a trick to using treats and I would suggest that everyone wishing to use them gets the DVD. It will be so beneficial to you to developing a true heart connection with your horse.

Time and again I see problems with people using treats and it's all down to how the horse perceives the treating. If he sees that you are gifting him, then it's fine. It's not so good however when he thinks that he took it from you. Just which way he sees this has a strong bearing on how he perceives himself in the pecking order in the herd comprising the two of you.

If you want a really quick, simple tip on using treats it is .... don't let him have it if he is rude!

Change the Focus: Using Grain to Encourage a Horse from the Barn

This question comes from Danny in Alabama, who is faced with a challenge perhaps many of you experience with new horses. The way to deal with it is similar to the way you might deal with a child that is upset; you change their focus. Read on to see what Danny asks and what I recommend. Hope it helps!

I have acquired a couple of horses because their owner could not feed them. I have ridden all my life and never had this problem. You have to fight these horses away from the barn; I mean it is a rodeo every time. What can be done? Thanks.

Thanks for your question. Here's what you need to do.

Grain your horses away from the barn. Place some grain on the trail that you will be riding along and hand lead them there. When the horses get the idea that it is good to receive the grain away from the barn, you can then ride them out to where the grain is located. This should fix the problem.

Here is the exercise that will make this easier to accomplish from the saddle. Point the horse in the direction you want to go. Get him to stand there on a dropped rein. If he turns his head one way or the other, use the rein to place his head back on center and again drop the rein. Gently ask him to go forward. When he takes a few steps willingly then ask him to stop and when he will stop and stand on a dropped rein return him to the barn. Repeat. The idea is that the horse learns that leaving the barn on your request gets him back to the barn.

As you progress with this exercise, every time you take a small trip away from the barn make sure to increase the trip further away each time. The horse should change his attitude because of this exercise and the grain he is receiving as he goes along the trail. A horse will naturally go where he is looking if you wait it out.

A demonstration of this is loading your horse into a trailer; if you take a horse that doesn't want to load into a trailer and you focus on keeping the horse on looking inside the trailer he will eventually walk in on his own. The trick is giving an adequate amount of time and keeping the horse calm.

When you ask a horse to do anything there has to be something in it for him, a "carrot." The only carrot you are offering your horse at this point is the horse's desire to get out of the battle. Get rid of the battle and find a better carrot. Make the carrot the destination itself. By changing the focus, you will be amazed at the results!

This may take some time but it will work. Good luck. I know that in this process, you will figure out a little different approach and we would love to hear back from you on what you did and how you accomplished what works.

RACEHORSES

The Abuse of Living Like Kings

Recently, I heard of the unfortunate, tragic end of the life and career of *Eight Belles,* a fabulous racehorse. I was struck by the comments of several people interviewed about the event and I realized that I felt absolute outrage at some of these comments.

First, I remember the reporter asking a gentleman about the race and the ethics of horse racing. The gentleman said that horses "love racing" and "she (*Eight Belles*) especially would have given her life to be able to race." He went on to say that the horses at the track were "treated like kings and had a great life thanks to the racing industry."

I know that sounds like a great life, but wait a minute here. A king has the right to make choices and live as he chooses. A horse would no more choose that kind of life than I would choose to live in a prison cell, no matter how beautifully it was decorated or how many servants I had. Horses in their wild and natural setting prefer the company of other horses not humans - company they choose. They like to roam free in large open spaces whilst grazing and foraging for food. No matter how well cared for a racehorse may be, this is not the life he would choose for himself.

This idea that horses are treated ethically is something that is thrown around so casually. In fact, the life span of many racehorses is cut short by slaughter when injuries force them out of 'productive work'. If they can and do recover from a race related injury, they may be able to do another job. However they are not trained for any other job after racing and the burden and expense of that training falls on the next potential owner. Their owners show no care if a race related injury means a horse is unable to continue a career in racing.

And what about the hundreds, maybe thousands of horses that are simply not good enough to be successful as a racehorse? What happens to them? Where is their "royal treatment"? They probably end up at what they call "rescue centers." Horse rescue is increasing as the numbers of 'unusable' horses goes up. Charity is being provided to the animals discarded by wealthy owners who have no accountability other than cutting their costs. We frown on dog owners that don't take responsibility for their animals. Why don't we feel the same about horses?

I think that racehorse owners are getting away with a lot since there are no provisions made for the care and housing of horses that they purchased but no longer wish to maintain. If I were a racehorse, I would want a guaranteed retirement with health benefits for all my efforts and the risks I was taking with my health.

Each year over 13,000 thoroughbreds are produced for racing purposes. How many of those are living the great life of a king? I venture to say the number is in the hundreds. Racing may be one of the greatest contributors to the abuse of horses, indirectly if not directly.

I think horse racing needs more accountability. If the owners had to pay for the long-term care of horses, then we may get to see some of the following beneficial steps being taken:

- Breeding programs that produce better quality horses that can race with fewer breakdowns;
- Training programs that increase more personal well-being and support the emotional life of young horses at the track;
- Racing older, more mature horses;
- Providing racing environments that support the horses... better racing surfaces;
- Responsibility for rehabilitation training; and
- Care, housing and provision after retirement

Racehorses: Saving the True Spirit (Part One)

After my last article on horse racing *The Abuse of Living like Kings*, I was asked *"What could we do to help stop the abuse and neglect in this industry?"* I personally would like it if horses were not whipped to the finish line, not raced at such a young age or indeed not raced at all!

It is not a new subject that the racehorse industry needs to bring more well-being to horses. I love horses and it is my desire to connect horses and humans together in harmony. Not the way we want, but the way that benefits the horse.

I will start by suggesting we support our local rescue centers and all active programs and individuals, who are taking the responsibility to care for these horses. There are so many wonderful people saving racehorses. They are self-directed angels out in the field putting their whole lives into facilitating better treatment of racehorses. Check with them and find out how you can help. Send thank you cards or cards of support to these centers and individuals and/or send a donation of any size to let them know that their efforts are appreciated.

Another thing that someone might want to do is put together a list of all the local non-profit organizations that are rehabilitating and taking in retired racehorses. This is something that has not been put together that

I am aware of and would be a great resource. If you do know of such a list, please let me know.

If you plan to get a horse for your pleasure, you could instead save a retired racehorse and adjust your pleasure around your horse's needs. My bonding rituals will give you a great connection whether you ride or not. They are every day rituals horses share with each other to bring a sense of belonging, harmony and well-being to the horse's spirit.

I hope what I write inspires you and as a result may help many more horses to be saved. Major positive changes can happen from a simple act of asking.

It brings to mind the book by Esther and Jerry Hicks, '*Ask and it is Given*'. As I see it, once the question is asked the energy to resolve it comes forward effortlessly; to quote them, "Simple focus brings solutions." What we can add besides our support to the rescue centers is to visualize a world of compassion and a desire to bring well-being to horses. Don't visualize passively; really get into it, feel it, taste it, live it, dream and talk about it. Keep a journal. The passion you generate brings energy for making change. Try to stay away from resentment and negativity.

One thing I know, being a practical person, is that shame and anger puts up firewalls of resistance to the people and situations we want to change like it does with horses. I avoid shame and blame because it inhibits the natural flow of source energy that will support this change. I would also like to suggest that if the subject makes you very angry, it might help you to become more active. Your anger may be calling you into action to fight for the cause. You will know this to be true if your anger subsides from your involvement. My advice is to let go of the negative energy, it will only hold progress back. I have noticed that people don't get upset at the things they cannot change...like gravity, etc.; they only get upset at what they can change. Be the change.

Feel solutions and let the dance begin. When I am training a horse, I don't focus on the problem, instead, I make a connection with him. This way the problem disappears.

After helping the rescue centers the next thing to do is to put visualization to work as an everyday practice. Anger helps to gain momentum but it cannot achieve your goal until you release it. The first thing to do is get really clear about what it is that you don't want so you can let go of the negative energy and facilitate the changes you would like to see. Once you are clear and in a positive space, see that the change is happening right now! In this space, you are a powerhouse for change.

We can visualize that the racehorse industry cares more for their horses than making money or placing bets. We can visualize that the breeding programs start breeding racehorses like the Arabian breeding programs in Poland. They were bred for temperament, stamina and heart before speed. They did not breed horses that broke down on the track. Can you believe that our country does? We could visualize that horses are not raced as young as they are. We could visualize the owners falling in love with their horses and keeping them forever. I like that one a lot. We could visualize the racehorses going on to live out happy productive lives. We could visualize that no one is interested in racing horses anymore because they see it is inhumane to have such a sport. Bravo!!! Or, horses get to run and enjoy it as much as humans and stay sound with a long life provided by their owners. This would be my dream!

The treatment of horses is getting better every day. Years ago, it was common to see horses kept in tie stalls. It was worse than the stalls that confine horses today. If a horse was not working, he was tied up in a dark barn, maybe by himself, until he died of old age or was shot. Sometimes a bullet would not be wasted on a horse and it was left to die with no remorse or gratitude for his service in life. Or if a horse fell in the field from the exhaustion of pulling a plow or failed to perform correctly, it was whipped to death like we saw in the movie *'Gone with the Wind'*. Horses were ridden on long journeys and eaten along the way as a matter of practice. We have come a long way since then.

It is more important to see our progress than to focus on negatives. I am told that It is part of the laws of quantum physics that our thoughts create our reality. Keeping positive thoughts and feelings on what we would like for the horses rather than what we want stopped will bring positive solution.

This is why I do not fix problems in the training of horses; I focus on connection and friendship to open the door to a true partnership with my horses. This way the problem is fixed through forming a bond, trust and respect.

Evolution, everyday deeds, a positive outlook and vigilant focus will help the racehorse industry to bring the horse a better lifestyle and support them throughout their natural lives. I see changes every day and I hope this is of some comfort.

Racehorses: Saving the True Spirit (Part Two)

I'd like to continue today with my thoughts on racehorses and how we can help them. One big problem I see is how to get people to give up a lifestyle of joy and celebration around the love of horseracing when its history is full of legends, heroes and greats. There are many honorable traditions of horseracing and many families live these traditions, worship famous trainers, jockeys and horses that love to run like *Eight Belles*.

Let's not forget about the money, personal self worth, joy and drama that surround the racing industry. It seems like a mammoth undertaking to try and change it, doesn't it? Much like riding a horse towards a jump that you know you can't make and on the other side is the unknown - could be it's an eight-foot drop ending in a hopeless crash. It's pretty scary and maybe the smart thing would be to stop trying. But you can't do that either because of the anger, guilt and gnawing in your stomach.

So when these overwhelming feelings come up, what can we do? We need to start fresh every day. Remember our resources are strong, our focus is united and connecting with others doubles our resources for change. Keep doing what we are doing, by writing on blogs and spreading the word, it's so powerful. Blogs have the same power or more as our folk singers of the 40's, 50's and 60's had in affecting change.

Right now we are creating the energy for change from our passion and connection on this blog and all the blogs around the world. If we just look at the size of the problem, it weakens our ability to be effective. Horses never lose their spirit, so let's not lose ours and draw upon the pool of resources we have. I like to think we are on the cutting edge of bringing more compassion to this planet and the first step is seeing the change right here and now. Imagine what it would look like in a world where 'shoulds' and 'should nots' are not needed to keep horses safe because they already receive the love and proper care they deserve. Just imagine that!!! It may seem silly but imagine it anyway.

Please write to me, either by comment or email, with your view of what it would look like. Be silly and joyful. The more joyful energy you bring the more magnetic support you will draw to our cause. Pass on your own stories to others, make movies and write books. Forming clubs that bring connection to support horses is the greatest strength we have.

We can also offer our services free to racetracks: Homeopathy, Bach Flower remedies, massage, acupressure, grooming, companionship, communication and chiropractics. Whilst performing these services, don't point angry fingers; just offer service and suggestions that "might" be put into action.

If you are an artist, paint a picture of a horse being honored and what it would look like. Make scrapbooks and buy horse art from these artists. We need to support each other. Listen to horse music and write songs. If you are a writer, write a book, blog or article.

Shine your light and tell people horses are the reason your light is shining. Go to the track and hand out leaflets on anything you are passionate about but don't point fingers. Make friends and share what you can to make a difference when you are passing out your leaflets.

We all have something to offer if we choose to be in "action". It is important to notice the things that are getting better. Many tracks have better surfaces for the horses to run on. Many people aren't going to the tracks because they feel it is unfair to the horses. Many changes have been made to benefit racehorses because of the shift in consciousness we have already put into practice. By building the compassion in our hearts for the people causing the abuse, we create more willingness in them to bring a better quality of life to their horses. It is all about compassion and noticing that the smallest adjustment can make big changes. It creates good Karma.

When I am training a horse and ask for a new behavior, I will look for something small; a soft eye or just the tiniest response, however odd.

Then I am delighted and I give him a cookie and let him graze as a reward. The next day he performs like he knew it all the time. I know the power of subtle changes. This shift in small degrees needs to be acknowledged for the seed to grow.

Being aware of subtle changes, you will discover that the path of least resistance is the quickest path for permanent change. You might ask how this is any different than just standing by and doing nothing. It is different because of our intention, our positive thoughts and feelings and because creating alignment with others has great power. It is like my first Ritual. When I align myself with a horse by sharing space with him doing nothing, it gives meaning to the rest of my Rituals and brings out a horse's desire to dance with me. We need people who are in the "action journey" saving individual horses right now and we need more people to hold the space for them. Both of these roles bring more aid and support to each another.

Anything you can dream up is better than what horses are experiencing right now. Not just racehorses, but all horses in general.

I will conclude my thoughts in my next article on how we can help racehorses by looking at the best thing we can do looking ahead to provide the best long term solution.

Racehorses: Saving the True Spirit (Part Three)

In this article I would like to conclude my thoughts on how we can help racehorses by looking to the future.

The strong permanent change we can make is to guide children to be compassionate and caretakers of horses. A great way to start with children is to ask them what the horse's world looks like when humans are supportive to their needs. Go to schools and ask this question. Remember, ask and it is given!!! This is something I have done in the past and you might consider the same in order to facilitate change.

I believe I made some profound changes when I took my miniature stallion, Lad, into schools. I would feed him up with food so he would poop and this was a great hit with the kids. I took a magnifying glass with me to show children what a horse looked like up close. It also gave me the opportunity to create compassion as I told them of the abuse and also the proper way to care for horses. I gave them the opportunity to experience the horse's hooves, tongue, teeth, heartbeats, gut sounds and poop on the ground (that got lots of laughs). I explained that horses have feelings, emotions and families. That they care for their families and suffer when separated from each other because they are herd animals. I shared with them that respect for the horse means that when he bucks or pulls on the bit it's for a reason. Maybe he doesn't want to be ridden... maybe he doesn't understand the communication. We have to address our responsibility to get a voluntary performance and not take things by force.

I knew I had made changes because of the compassionate questions the children asked me later. These children knew nothing about horses and by the end of the hour, they were asking questions that showed their deep caring. I had opened their thoughts of hope that horses are cared for properly. Most kids after only an hour told me if they ever had a horse, they would take good care of his emotions and physical well-being and give him a proper environment and only ride their horse if the horse would enjoy it. I had many of them say "If I have a horse I will keep it forever and never ride it, horses are my friends."

I believe if we focus on developing this attitude in our children, in 30 years there will be no cruelty in horseracing – there is even the possibility that there will be no horse racing at all. Visualize what you want and it will happen.

I remember telling a friend of mine, Stuart, about wanting to have a school of horsemanship. I told him my dream, I wrote it down and for some reason the first things I wanted for my school were church bells and a fountain. Seems like such an odd thing to want church bells for a horsemanship center but it just popped into my head. Then as I heard them in my imagination, I experienced the subtle joy of listening and feeling how connected a person could get to all things on earth as the resonance of sound lifted my heart upwards to a heightened awareness of freedom and harmony. I know in these moments it is easy to connect with horses.

As you recall and coincidentally, the racehorse that started all these discussions was called *Eight Belles*! I can still feel now the energy of *Eight Belles* in my heart encouraging me to help others to connect to the true spirit of horses through gratitude and responsibility. When I find the bells for my school (I know now how many I need!), I will hear them ringing and know that we will continue to keep *Eight Belles*' spirit in our hearts and be vigilant for the future of racehorses.

CHAPTER SEVEN
STORIES

SELECTION OF READER STORIES

Horse Tales from the Mountain - Part One

I am delighted to present the first in a series of stories from Margaret. I have asked her if she wouldn't mind sharing some of her journey with us as she gets to know her mare, Autumn, in the 230 acres they and 30 other horses share up there in the mountains in northern California. Margaret seems to experience the same joy as I do from the simple pleasures to be found in nature and her stories bring a smile to my heart. I hope they do to yours too.

Last Saturday was a real neat morning for us. I couldn't sleep and decided to head to the barn around 5:30am. I found Autumn in the lower meadow of the pasture which looks like the edge just falls off into the red-wooded mountains below us. A thunderstorm the night before lit up a bunch a forest fires and a light veil of smoke hung in the valley. I could just barely see the outline of the full moon. I was sitting there, Autumn grazing away beside me when the sunlight behind me lit up the smoky haze in an orange glow. I turned to look at Autumn when I noticed that the moon and the sun were completely parallel to each other in the sky. It was like two old lovers catching a glimpse of each other in a crowd of people. It only lasted for a few minutes before they were torn apart but it was so cool. I felt lucky to have seen that with my best friend beside me.

A little after that I dozed off and woke up with Autumn standing with her head right over me while a bunch of her friends crept in close to me. I was a little alarmed and glad I didn't have a hoof wake me up but there was my baby standing guard. She wandered off as soon as I was awake and resumed her eating.

I've seen a bunch of Carolyn's YouTube videos. It's hypnotic to watch Carolyn and her horses work with each other. That magnetic bond is just unbelievable. I have just a smidgen of that with Autumn and I know how exhilarating it is, even if it lasts only for a short while. But I'll tell you, what you do with your horses is what I want to be able to do with Autumn and any horse I ever get to work with. I've been watching Panadero's DVDs and scouring them over and over again to see what I can do with Autumn right now. I did the treats and the bucket and didn't let her "take it" but kept my space until she lost interest and I let her have her little treats. She kept an eye on me the whole time she ate and when she was finished she was "hooked on" to me. It was like a relaxing way to accomplish the join up in a round pen without running in tight circle running. She just followed me around forwards and backwards.

We've had a few funny things happen the past week. I've just been sneaking in little bits of time here and there because work has been busy; I hate not having enough time with her. Anyhow, her boyfriend horse, Opi, has been chasing her away from me when I come out in the pasture. She'll start walking up to me and he'll just run up to her biting her on the butt and hocks until she walks away all floppy eared and sad. I'm a pushier mare when it comes to my Autumn time and I'll chase him off and she'll just hide behind me, all 16 hands of her. Sometimes, in the mornings when I go to check on her I can't find either one of them with their normal herd. I swear he's hiding her!

She's really such a neat horse. I can tell she really loves me. I just found some old scrap books I made at about 10 years ago and found all these letters I wrote to my horse Flicker and they all had the line. "I love

Flicker. I know Flicker loves me" and they cracked me up. Twenty years later I'm writing the same things.

I have one neat story that happened a few months ago. I decided to take Autumn on a hike to the top of the mountain for some ocean views. We just were making our way down a narrow path; on one side is about a six foot straight drop that connects with a steep hill and on the other side is a big pond. The width of the path is about six feet wide. We had just gotten to the middle of the path when Autumn hit the brakes, and I heard the sound of 20-30 sets of hooves storming up the hill. We had nowhere to go. My mind slowed and reviewed what was about to happen. A herd of 30 horses were coming at us and our only options were to jump or swim. But before a plan of action could be made Autumn arched her body around me, head tucking me in, those big, beautiful draft legs anchoring themselves into place. The horses sped by in bay, sorrel, palomino and painted blurs. They splashed through the pond, balanced on the edge of the drop off and crashed into Autumn, rocking her body as she kept me tucked in safe next to her. When it was all over my heart was pounding and I was shaking like a leaf. I looked at Autumn and just knew that she just saved my life. She protected me. She kept her head on her shoulders when most horses would have kicked me in the ass as they were high-tailing it out of there. I guess that is why it is so important to me to work with Autumn in a way that is respectful of her, that keeps her spirit and her heart. I always want Autumn to have that love for me; enough to save me from being trampled on a trail or in life. I love Autumn. And Autumn loves me! (it still cracks me up to write that again!)

Horse Tales from the Mountain - Part Two

This article is the second in our series from Margaret and her best friend Autumn.

Well, I've been waiting for the big chapter two of our mountain tales to come to me and I think I'm looking too hard. I think that's my major problem with myself. I'm always waiting for that big epiphany, that moment that just transcends all others but sometimes they're so small you can miss them when they are right in front of you. If you're waiting for your horse to start side passing at liberty you might miss the moment when he's standing next to you breathing deep into your ear.

A few weeks ago I took Autumn for a walk in the woods. I led her to our turning around point, took her halter off and we walked freely along together. I felt like the luckiest girl alive, just me and my best friend walking side by side in lace patterned sunlight underneath the trees, and then her little ears pricked up and she trotted off down the road. I felt like I was just dumped and walked back past the shadows.

Twenty minutes later, I found Autumn grazing with her buddies, not at all concerned. I just stood, looked at her and in my sunken down thoughts asked her if she enjoys coming along with me. I turned around to leave and she lifted her head right above my shoulder and breathed deep into my ear. It silenced the world and spoke to me like the sea and the wind. There weren't words but there was something in those deep breaths that Autumn told me not to worry. It was so strange and clear but not spoken, just understood. It was a message that was kind, caring, nurturing, safe and peaceful. I listened to her. I stopped worrying. I don't know how long I stood there, probably only seconds, but it made a memory to last throughout my life.

There's something about a horse when they let you listen to or feel their breath. The other night, I sat in her stall while I wrote in my journal and she just stopped eating (very rare). She stood above me and just breathed into my hair. It was chilly that night as the fog rolled over the sunset and her warm breath blowing above me warmed my whole body.

She did this for a few minutes until she decided to give me a new hairdo with some horsey, snot-holding gel and went back to her food. That's when it occurred to me. They call today's top horsemen, "Horse Whisperers" but I think the term is wrong. It's the horses that whisper. The "Horse Whisperers" are the ones that are listening to what the horses tell them. It's the greatest horsemen that listen. Horses are talking to us; they are so quiet but always trying. I am trying harder than ever to give Autumn the chance to speak. I'm working my hardest to quiet all the chit chat in my mind so as to give Autumn the silence she needs to speak to me. I will be listening for her whispers for the rest of our lives.

Horse Tales from the Mountain - Part Three

The days are now getting shorter at the ranch. The once overflowing heart-shaped pond has shrunk into a lumpy looking potato. As the summer passed, Autumn and I watched the purple forest clover turn to the carpeting sunshiny buttercups in the meadows, which eventually fell underneath the waving oceans of daises. These were later pushed out by the prickly purple thistles and now the Queen Anne's lace is trying its' hardest to dress up the dry and dusty pasture. The cool autumn winds are starting to rattle the skeletons of the headless thistles that I think Autumn had a big part in plucking this season, and the mountains sit crisp, waiting for the winter rains to fall.

I.

Our days together in the pasture this summer have surely brought Autumn and I closer. I watched her friend Bob, a brown paint, who showed her the ropes in the pasture, move away and I felt her broken heart when she would call for him and the pasture fell quiet to her echoes. I watched a new summer fling with Copper come and go like the flowers, when he dumped her for CC, a pretty little sorrel from Texas. Now, Autumn has a heart-struck lover named Willy, who keeps her in his herd with hearts dancing in his eyes. She grumps around under his smothering presence but if he wanders to another, she creeps on over to catch his attention. Opi is still her buddy who searches out adventure in the wind that carries across the mountains and tells him where to lead their herd.

Poncho, from their barn, has just started going out on pasture and they're showing him around the block. It's a major pool party when the four of them get into the pond - water is splashing - they're crashing into each other as they roll around in it and they finish up by taking a long drink as they cross to the other side. It's so cool to watch them and the little lives they live. I can't ever imagine keeping her in a little pen ever again.

Autumn goes out in the morning (she's been wanting to come in at night to eat more now that the pasture is dead - she's a growing Belgian you know!) and calls to her friends until she finds them. They nibble around, they snooze in the sunshine until they get too warm, then they hike it up to their favorite potato-shaped pond for a splash and roll and then they wait for dinner time. I love that they decide what they are going to do for the day. It makes them so much happier when you want to take them out to do whatever you want to do.

Sooooooooooooooo, I did something the other night that was one of the best things that ever happened in my life! I had taken a class that day, I went shopping at the mall for a while, I went to the bookstore and when I was done, it was around 8pm. I decided whilst driving home, "What the hell, I'm going to go see Autumn". I pulled up to the barn, grabbed a pocket knife and skirted down the dark, little path hoping that there wasn't a mountain lion ready to pounce onto my paranoid self. It was foggy down in the meadow but the moon glowed three days shy of being full. I could make out silhouettes of horses a few strides away but their grazing lips gave them away before their shadows.

I whispered for Autumn, not wanting to wake the ranch owner up. My plan was not to go into the woods to find her if she wasn't in the pasture. I was starting to give up hope, nearing the forest, when the moonlight caught her blaze floating through the fog. Her eyes held more light than the moon and the excitement of being with my horse crept inside me. She stood on the hillside and the little girl in me, who had watched the "Black Stallion" probably more times than is healthy, grabbed a handful of mane and attempted to swing up on her bareback. I failed miserably and ended up kicking the poor girl in the sides twice. She stood there with the forgiving patience of a saint and I gave her a hug and we headed for the gate.

But before we got there, she stopped next to a slight embankment where I was above her in perfect sliding-a-leg-over-her-back position. Well I did! I got on my Baby Autumn! There we were in the middle of a dream. I pinched myself and she turned and touched my left dangling foot and then my right. It wasn't a dream. I grabbed two handfuls of her thick secure mane. She began to walk and I held onto her mane like it was the first time I had ever been on a horse. I was squeaking and laughing without worrying about it.

She stopped again to check out my legs and even bit my shoe. I sat there then and even as I sit here now and can still feel her big warm body beneath me. I leaned down and hugged her big, thick neck and her mane coarsely rubbed against my cheek. I patted her flank behind me; I looked at her perked little ears and rolled my little feet in the air next to her sides.

The moonlight's glow in its foggy, grey light caused her mane and tail to glisten. All around us in the glow of the fog, I rode my best friend Autumn in the clouds of a real life dream. She walked us to the pasture gate, where I gave her one last hug and stole every second on her to keep forever in my memories. I slid off her, not wanting to ever get off. I hugged her, patted her and just bounced around like a little kid after her first pony ride. Autumn followed alongside me the whole time in the dark glow back to the barn with the two of us sparkling from our adventure in the clouds.

Autumn - The Moody Horse!

I would like to share with you an email I received from Margaret, about her horse Autumn who has been causing her a few problems by demanding treats in a somewhat grumpy fashion.

Now as you read Margaret's story, think about how you can take the advice I gave to Margaret, adapt it and use it with your horse if he is presenting you with similar problems. A lot of horse training is about using your imagination and coming up with solutions that are fun for both of you.

Sorry I didn't write you back right away after our phone call but I had to leave town for a surf contest. The contest wasn't too much fun as it was the first storm of the season and the waves were too big and too moody. I got really excited when you made the comparison to a surfer riding a wave and working with a horse. It's so true. The ocean teaches the lesson a little better then a horse; she is the biggest thing on the planet and there's no changing her ways.

So, I took your advice with Autumn about leading her to the treats instead of handing them over to her when she demanded. When I was working with her at liberty, every time I asked her to trot, she'd pin her ears, shake her head and look like a big old grump. I never once thought she was chasing me down for a treat. I would give her a treat to reward her for trotting next to me when asked but I didn't make the connection that she thought she had to come up to me in that bossy manner to get it.

Instead, I tried what you said about bringing her to a magically placed treat that only I knew the location of. I took her into the arena and we worked on her walking with me without the grumpy ears to a treat. I would stop her when she would put them back and then she'd give me the pocket nod and I'd just wait and say ears. At first she didn't know what I was up to so I had to figure out a way to let her know what I wanted.

So, at first I let her come up all grumpy for a treat just to perk her interest. Then after that, when she came up to me she had to stop until her ears went up. We had to stop a few times but it didn't take her long to make the connection, "go to where Margaret is and she'll show me where the cookies are". She was so excited to follow me to the next spot; she was like a little kid at Easter looking for Easter eggs. She could hardly wait until I asked her to come to me at a new spot. It didn't take long before she had happy ears all the time and her eyes were sparkling.

At one point, she came to see me and I produced a magic carrot. She hesitated and looked at me in disbelief, as if I had just pulled a quarter out from behind her ear. The funny thing for me was that it seemed too easy and that I had too much fun doing it. I almost had trouble believing that I was teaching her something and we were both enjoying it. It sounds crazy, but every time I think I've worked with a horse I always have a creeping anxiety that I'm not going to be able to get the horse to do it again. I've done the exercise over a few more times and I haven't seen grumpy ears since then. I've been gone a few days and look forward to doing it again. I haven't asked her to trot to a magical treat destination yet but I think tomorrow I'll try it out.

Bonding with Jasper - The Rescue Horse

This letter is from a lady from Northern California with the lovely name of Indigo. The reason for putting it here was twofold. One is to help people understand that they need to take more time on the relationship with their horse and that training is more than a 20 minute experience. Indigo's story demonstrates this beautifully. The second reason was that it also illustrates that there is this kind of field of dreams and connections, as you will see when you read the whole story. I hope you enjoy it as much I did.

Jasper was adopted on October 1, 2006. I just found out the exact date because I finally was able to complete the requirement for him to be out of probation with the BLM (for me to be able to halter him). He first lived in a little pipe corral, the kind specified by the BLM: tiny solitary confinement. There was a non-intimate interface with the herd; sometimes they hang around the gate some fifteen feet from Jasper's original corral. He was so freaked out. If you got within ten feet of him, he would leap away as if shocked by a cattle prod. He was adopted as a first horse for a boyfriend. He has one eye with a reduced sclera, making him look even flightier than he really is.

Winter break rolled around and his adopter was heading south for a month. She asked me if I thought she should turn Jasper out into the 200-some-odd acres with the 25 other horses that lived out there. I, not knowing the rules of the adoption agreement and horrified by the space and conditions he was subjected to, said "Heck, yeah, let him out!"

One thing led to another and I ended up the proud "owner" of a wild horse. It could hardly pass as ownership in any way. It boiled down to me being responsible for paying his bills and following him around. I had been spending time with him before he was semi-officially transferred to me. My initial tactic, as it were, was to find the herd and observe them as a whole, noting how Jasper fitted in with them. The observation that gave me hope and fostered my belief that Jasper would in time come to trust humans, was that he fraternized with the friendly, outgoing and confident horses (and mules) in the herd.

When I did seek to initiate interaction with Jasper, I did it with the intention of showing him, through consistency and repetition that I was aware of and respectful of his boundaries. If I breached them, I immediately backed off, and acknowledged my mistake. I would bring him tubs of grain and fend off the entire herd while he stood eating. He quickly learned my waving whip-arm was not aimed at him but was rather defending his space so he could have such a tasty treat. It was a little triumph when I was one day waving my scarf trying to get him to move away and he simply looked at it, looked at me, and didn't move!

I allowed myself and Jasper the time it took for me to accomplish gaining his trust, getting to the point where I could, being very transparent with my intentions, approach and halter him without having to trick him. This took over a year! I was only able to visit Jasper once or twice a week and he was not dependent on me for any of his needs.

Jasper has such a strong sense of self that he would let me know if I was putting too much pressure on our developing line of trust. I remember two distinct times where he wheeled and kicked at me. I have been around a lot of different horses and been kicked at in a number of different situations with a wide range of distance between me and a horse. Never had I felt such power of personality in a warning kick, never had I been so acutely aware that a cognitive choice had been made to warn me with such a fair and clear idea of justice packed into it. I thanked Jasper heartily for sparing my body and thanked my person for being able to recognize the interaction for what it was.

The second kick like that came not so long ago when we had passed the cliché milestone in our relationship where Jasper had allowed me to put a halter on his head. I was back to doing some liberty stuff but I had popped out of being present and was thinking with my "horseperson" filter, the one that says we make horses do what we want and I was being a bit demanding. Jasper issued his warning with a dose of up yours and a measure of don't get bigger than your breeches and a reminder that we are supposed to be doing this together.

I have the biggest prize that a horse can ice a trust cake with: I have Jasper's interest, I have piqued his curiosity. The goal of putting a halter on was imposed by society. Jasper and I were both subject to it. It gave me some structure, some framework to move about in, in all the formlessness of this challenging adventure I had undertaken.

My triumphs were small, like Jasper hesitating and choosing to stay rather than leave. Like Jasper finally relaxing enough near me to chomp his jaw. Some things came so much faster for him than for other horses, like him drawing towards me when I asked him to with my body language. I spent lots of time crouching on my haunches in front of him, hiding the bits of apple and carrot he had come to expect and love in my folded arms. He would root around in between my arms, pushing his nose in the circle of my chest and arms. He let me touch his muzzle first, with the whole hand feeding thing and the mouth-handedness of a horse. It surprised me that the first place he really let me pet him was at the base of his neck. That was always my favorite, softest place on a horse when I was a girl. There were times Jasper would pretend to be looking for a treat still just to prolong the neck scratches that he initially demanded concurrent feeding for.

There were also times when I got pretty dejected, wondering what the heck I had gotten myself into with this stubborn and proud dun gelding. Without fail, on my next visit with Jasper, he would make a leap of allowance that would buoy my hope and determination.

I can, with some degree of consistency, now touch Jasper on his face, neck down to his knees, on his back and rump. I can approach him with halter and lead rope, dropping the rope on the ground as I open the halter up to slip over his nose. Jasper comes, stops, backs and yields his hind end at liberty. He will execute circles around me, but does not love to yield his shoulder. If he decides to leave, I can almost always "catch" his energy and convince him to come back to me.

I found a place to move to that I feel is as good as or better than his current situation. The trick is going to be getting him into a trailer. I finally feel that our bond is getting strong enough to withstand the discomfort of a trailer ride and I am prepared for there to be some backsliding in his trust of me as a result of his displeasure. I know that many horses are okay with riding in trailers but you know that his first experiences with the beasts were filled with fear and pain. My next step is to convince Jasper that he will be safe if he makes his way into a corral. Now that my requirement of haltering the boy is met, I can leave that be and work at liberty, the most fun and evocative. It is amazing how quickly my old mode of operating comes back when I have a rope in my hands!

Jasper lives at the same ranch that Margaret's draft mare, Autumn, lives. I admire your work greatly; your book, *Naked Liberty* was pivotal in opening my eyes and helping me to be brave at being a "weirdo" in horse-land. There are so many more details and ideas that I could convey, I just kind of wrote what flowed out. I hope I piqued your interest.

Rowan: the Rescue Horse

This heart-warming and touching story comes from a lady called Dannielle in Ontario, Canada who wrote to me about a rescue horse she took in called Rowan.

I am so happy to have stumbled upon your story and books. You were part of my journey for a deeper understanding to how I was feeling and my relationship to certain horses. I suppose my deepest and most Intense relationship was to the farm that I consider myself the keeper of. After the raising of a severely mentally handicapped son whom I cared for at home until he was 21, while working full time and caring for the farm, I knew it was time for me. I had several spiritually enlightening experiences while on a trip to Ireland and came home open and ready to truly listen and embrace the journey I was on. I have had many horses on the farm - rescues and well trained ones - and the though the well-trained are a pleasure to be around, it was the misunderstood who attracted me most.

Recently my business partner rescued an abused horse at a local auction from the hands of the meat dealer. At the time I was very annoyed with him because I could not afford another but this little mare has come into my heart and I have never felt more bonded to a truly dysfunctional horse in my life. I am in love and as a result of that love I have started a line of stable accessories which are of spiritual design; switched the focus of my stable to Intelligent Horsemanship and discovered a whole new zest for life. She has rescued me and has accepted me as a passenger and although there is no formal training yet we hack the trail together; playing and breathing in each other. Together we explore the unbeaten path. I think it and she goes, never have I felt this with a horse before. Thank you for the inspiration.

Rowans Story:

I was not happy with the news. One more mouth to feed, one more untrained horse to deal with. I had sent them off to buy a plough and they came back with a horse. I was determined to stay mad at my friend, Tim, this time. I got the news from my daughter that they had arrived at the stable with a new horse and I was on my way up. Tim met me outside the stable while the others stayed in with the horse. He knew exactly how to get to me, calm me. All he had to do was tell me the only one bidding on her was him and the meat guy. He asked me to keep an open mind that he thought we would be a good match of personalities. Ha!!! What did he know?

My first sight of her was on crossties, two young men trying to get the burrs out of her mane and a forelock, that looked like a unicorn horn. The whole time she is trying to bite them. Eyes bulging, wild, and striking out with her feet when the mood came on, and pig squeals emitting from her mouth. Yes sir, every horsewoman's dream. I looked at Tim like he had lost his mind. My best friend was trying to get me killed for sure. Then he has the nerve to say "I think she likes women better. You will get along with her, I know it". I closed my lips around one of my snide comments. Instead I held back, gave in, and went over to her.

Looking at her with a critical eye, fear etched all over her face. Underlying that was also the look that said "You can't break my spirit". I put my hand on her neck and asked her to settle down and to my astonishment she did. We had a little chat about her behavior, and that I wouldn't hurt her. I felt for her but was determined to remain aloof. Too many horses have broken my heart. Too many had seriously hurt my cash flow. The other two culprits made quick exits rushing home to their wives leaving us to deal with this golden horse filled with fear. I asked Tim to put HIS horse in her stall, she wouldn't go in. Great, stubborn and defiant, just what we need. So, Elise, my dear daughter, took over and she went in ok. She had on a halter that was too small and digging into her head but obviously there was no way we were getting it off that night and I was too tired to think about how we would manage this one.

The plan of action was to NOT focus on all the bad and just assume she would respond to good. She didn't let me down. There was a light in her eyes and she really did trust women more. Over the weeks she stopped the striking and pig squealing. The frequency of "tasting" people was improving and she was happier with a new halter on. She decided she really liked feeding time but really wasn't terribly patient in a stall.

It was time to start working her in the round pen. Never have I had a horse respond in the round pen the way she did, or to the lunge whip for that matter. She turned in and looked straight at me. I flicked the whip, she threw her head in the air. I flicked it again and she struck at it. This was not going well. I tried again and she grabbed it in her mouth, THAT was a little unnerving. On to using a rope and praying she would be OK with it. I had to walk her around the pen to get her moving, but she didn't try to taste me or kill me. I thanked her profusely and called it a day. There was such a spark to her and she moved so well. I was intrigued. She spoke to something deep within me. Something misunderstood.

Rowan's days were progressing normally. She had found her place within the rhythm of the herd. Days outside, and nights in. She was now being handled by Tim without any bouts of violence. Progress required patience and respect. She tolerated nothing less.

It was spring now. You know those perfect days when the sun shines, the mud is drying and all of the horses are snoozing in the warmth after a long winter. I had been working around the stable when I looked into the paddock and saw her stretched, flat out in the hay strewn around the round bale in the field. She looked so calm and relaxed. Could that really be Rowan? Now, what is the first thought of any horsewoman when she sees her horse sunning itself like that? We fall back to our days of little girls dreaming of the perfect horse and snuggling up to it for a snooze. Crazy thoughts, for crying out loud we are talking about Rowan. The one who likes to "taste" people; but she looked so sweet and peaceful.

Yikes! Yes, I must be nuts because I wanted to believe in the good in her. To treat her as I do the rest of my herd. I decided to give her to opportunity to eat me! No, I wanted to give her the opportunity to be loved. It is what we all crave, so why should she be any different? I carefully opened the gate, and slowly walked in her general direction. There was that other voice in my head asking me what I was trying to prove. When I got close, I saw her eye open and look at me. I ignored her and sat five feet away in the hay. Her eyes were watching me but she stayed stretched out. I slowly inched closer, said a little prayer to the goddess and stretched out. After a little while, I felt her nose sniffing me

- thinking to herself - to taste or not to taste. I was praying for the latter. It worked. She stretched until she was touching me, sighed and relaxed and went back into a deep sleep. I was so relieved. There was such softness to her that something shifted in me. Of course by that time I was cold as the hay covered the remaining spring ice and the cold was coming through. I got up and so did she. She followed me.

That night I informed Tim that I had good news and bad news for him. He chose the bad first. I told him he no longer owned Rowan. He panicked thinking someone had come for her. I told him the good news was that she was mine. Maybe what I really meant was, I was hers. She had touched something in me that day. I had read somewhere that we see something of ourselves reflected in the horse we choose. I am on a journey with Rowan. I wonder what she will teach me about myself.

Companionship - The Guiding Sound

Sometimes I get totally unsolicited letters and emails from people who just want to share their similar view of the world. This post comes from a lady called Cindee, who wrote to me out of the blue last month. The story and pictures Cindee sent however are very close to my heart. Companionship is a one minded connection and horses share this too as you will read.

There is a field, with two horses in it. From a distance, each horse looks like any other horse. But if you stop your car, or are walking by, you will notice something quite amazing. Looking into the eyes of one horse will disclose that he is blind. His owner has chosen not to have him put down but has made a good home for him. This alone is amazing.

If you stand nearby and listen, you will hear the sound of a bell. Looking around for the source of the sound, you will see that it comes from the smaller horse in the field.

Attached to the horse's halter is a small bell. It lets the blind friend know where the other horse is so he can follow.

As you stand and watch these two horses, you'll see that the horse with the bell is always checking on the blind horse. The blind horse will listen for the bell and then slowly walk to where the other horse is, trusting that he will not be led astray.

When the horse with the bell returns to the shelter of the barn each evening, it stops occasionally and looks back, making sure that the blind friend isn't too far behind to hear the bell.

Like the owners of these two horses, God does not throw us away just because we are not perfect or because we have problems or challenges. He watches over us and even brings others into our lives to help us when we are in need.

Sometimes we are the blind horse being guided by the little ringing bell of those who God places in our lives. Other times we are the guide horse, helping others to find their way. Good friends are like that - you may not always see them but you know they are always there.

Please listen for my bell and I'll listen for yours. And remember; be kinder than necessary as everyone you meet is fighting some kind of battle.

Live simply; Love generously; Care deeply; Speak kindly...Leave the rest to God.

Picasso, the Friesian-Lipizzaner Gelding

Today, I want to share a story with you that was sent in by Katie from northern California. Katie's story just shows what can be done if you just go out and follow what's in my book and in my DVDs. You will see how much and how fast her relationship with her horse, Picasso, changed just by doing these simple *Waterhole Rituals*™. She also has a similar success with a couple of wild paint colts she was hired to gentle.

I have recently discovered your method. Wow, I am almost done with your book, and I just finished your DVD. I really love your approach and how you learned it. A few years ago, I adopted a BLM mustang, gentled, and started him. What an experience! I sadly had to sell him because I had no time, but he was my greatest teacher. After watching all of your rituals, I realized my mustang had taught those all to me! I was oblivious, but he knew what to do.

I currently have a six year old Friesian-Lipizzaner gelding named Picasso. I bought him as a yearling. We've had a great relationship until recently. I have been stressed because I am not working, and I haven't spent much time with him. Well, when I go out to see him now, he pretty much says in plain English, "I don't want to be with you." He used to play with me and we would dance, but that is not really happening now. And I know I made that happen. But I am on the road to fixing that with your help! It was very disheartening today when I went to play with him, and he ignored me and actually preferred to play with other horses. He was always so attentive and "easy". I took that for granted. Now I need to apply my mustang lessons and regain his love.

When I started to go back out to see him, he was a bit stand offish. Where he used to run next to me and play, he was now not interested.

So I got the DVD and listened to the book on my iPod. After feeling like I had a handle on your concepts, I went out to see Picasso. I believe I also mentioned that the mustang I used to own had made me go through all the *Waterhole Rituals™*. If I had applied what he had taught me to all horses, I would be more adept at it now.

Anyway, I took a book and went out to Picasso's pasture. His pasture is on a hill side with a flat area at the bottom. I went through his gate, where he happened to be standing. I said "hi" and walked passed him to go and sit down in the lower area. He did not come with me. He stayed where he was. I sat down there reading for about 45 minutes. He never came down, just looked at me. The next day I did the same thing. This time after about 20 minutes, he came down to see me. He sniffed me and then left. We did this little dance for three days. Then when I entered and went down to the bottom of his pasture, he came with me. I would go and sit down in his pasture, sometimes with a book, sometimes without a book. Either way I would sit there and just hang with him. After a couple of days of that, I brought his grain in and gave it to him while I sat nearby. I did that for a couple of days.

Once he was pretty well nosing me all the time, I took him to the arena and did the *Taking Space* ritual as seen on the video. We had been doing the hello ritual throughout this time as well. Today, when I did the *Taking Space* ritual, he tracked me the whole way around. I was never let out of his sight. It's quite rewarding to see that after two sessions of doing that ritual, he keeps eye contact! He still doesn't always follow me when food is near, so we are working on that.

Today when I enter his pasture, he is right next to me and will run down the hill with me and play at the bottom. I need to get someone to film that for me. He will still depart from me on occasion so I pull away from him as well. He comes back. We have not yet mastered what I guess I'd call a full bond where he will stay with me all the time. When in the arena, he still likes to go chat with the horses along the fence but if I ask him to come over to me, he will.

I also take Picasso on walks to the mail box. I live next door to where he is boarded, so we can walk to the mail box. I also did a little riding the other day in his halter. We've done that before, so he is pretty good. We cantered for the first time in halter and he was very good. More balanced than he was a month ago.

Rosalie: My Race Horse Dance Partner

This article is a story from Alessandra, a student of mine:

It is a hot summer morning and I am about two minutes away from "Dances with Horses", the ranch where my horse lives. Rosalie is a seven year old chestnut thoroughbred mare from the track. For the past year I have been training her using the Carolyn Resnick Method.

Rosalie is now well versed in Carolyn's Method and I have recently started to ride her. Each time we have done this, it has been a great experience for both of us and she has never shown any kind of resistance. We always ride in a large arena and a few times have done so bridleless. Our training program has a regular but very flexible schedule.

The most important thing is to be constantly aware of the relationship you have with the horse you are working with and choose your actions accordingly.

Carolyn's Method allows you and your horse to build a relationship with a solid foundation and a system of communication you can both depend on. This leads to teamwork, where the human leads and the horse follows as if it's his own idea. Because of this connection you then share, every area of work whether on the ground or in the saddle is accomplished effortlessly. From there, you can really tune your riding skills regardless of the equestrian discipline you choose to challe.nge yourself and your horse with.

When I arrive, Rosalie is eating her breakfast and doesn't openly acknowledge my presence. So I go about my routine, getting her feed and getting the tack ready, waiting to interact with her when she is more interested in our time together. I only have to wait a few minutes and she is hanging out on the side of her corral looking for me.

We always start each day by spending a few minutes together without interacting but giving each other time to express our state of mind. This time is very valuable for our performance together, whatever that may be.

Then we begin communicating with each other through what Carolyn calls the *Waterhole Rituals*™. This is what horses do in their own communities in the wild. Regardless of the time they have been apart, they always pick up their communication again this way.

If Rosalie doesn't show interest in following my lead, I use the *Waterhole Rituals* ™ further to re-establish my leadership. When I feel she is connected to me, I know I can do almost anything and she will want to do it with me. The few minutes of warm-up time with the rituals allow me to get connected with my horse so we can work in harmony from the beginning.

This past year has been a time of growth and change. My horse has gone from being a racehorse to learning to be part of a team that dances in harmony through any situation. I do not know where our limits are, we take new steps every day, finding new horizons, challenges and obstacles to jump together. Today may be learning the Spanish Walk or Piaffe together, tomorrow might be going out for the first time on a trail ride.

Today she looks like she is just waiting for me to start playing and so we do. After a few minutes of grooming I put the saddle on and lead her to the arena. We are connected. After a few minutes of working in hand and "single lining" (another part of Carolyn's Method) I feel it is time to ride. Rosalie is relaxed and I want her to experience the enjoyment that I do.

I ride her for about fifteen minutes, then I dismount and lunge her at walk, trot and canter. She is again following my lead and executing anything I ask of her. We do not need "turn out time", "chasing" or exhausting lungeing before working. Our state of connection creates the performance.

When we have this connection, Rosalie becomes my partner in a dance that we both enjoy and look forward to every time. She dances for me and my leadership dances in return. It is a shared experience.

What I have learned in the past year working with Carolyn is, I believe, of extreme importance for everyone who has horses in their life.

Thoroughbreds have always been my horse from the beginning with "Star" who was my first teacher, through the hundreds that I rode in races in Italy to Rosalie, the first horse I have owned.

Here's a sketch I did to celebrate the event, hope you like it!

A Little Squirrel Steals the Show in the Horse Training Area

I would like to share a fun story with you about a training session that I had with a thoroughbred mare whom I have worked with for some time, called Rosalie; a very, very wonderful mare to work with.

Well actually, the story is not really about Rosalie, it's about the ground squirrels that come around when Rosalie and I are training and I'm using treats. I use treats as part of my work with horses, not every session, but a lot of the time I work I do use them. I find that the horses learn faster that way and its makes it more enjoyable for the horse. It also helps to keep them polite, respectful and alert.

I bring the treats down to the training area in a container which I keep on the floor. The ground squirrels, which are true wild ground squirrels and a bit skittish, run off and hide when you first appear. But then when you are not looking, they run up and grab a little bit of food from the treat container and run off with it.

Well, in this particular training session with Rosalie, I noticed that one little ground squirrel seemed so frightened that all he could do was to stand up on the hill by the training area and watch all of the other ground squirrels come and steal the treats when I wasn't looking.

Then something really interesting happened, all of a sudden whilst I was working, this little ground squirrel ran out at my feet. I turned around and upon seeing me, instead of running away he squatted down in the dirt and wheeled around, I could not believe it.

I started walking towards him thinking that he would run away, but he did not. He started crawling towards me. This one little ground squirrel had figured out that the horses were doing tricks for treats and to get a treat he would try a trick. I reached down and gave him a treat. I put it at his feet; he picked it up, sat up and ate it. I continued training Rosalie, but he never ran away. He waited his turn for his treat when I was ready to give him one.

It was just a wonderful experience and now six months later and he is still with us.

Confidence and Clarity Above "Conventional" Horse Handling

I try to reply to comments people make on my article whenever I can but I thought I should reply to one I received this week in an actual post.

It was a lovely letter from a lady called Ellen and it brightened my day to hear how my work has such a strong and positive impact on people. I also hope that it will bring a sense of hope and direction to those out there who feel in their heart that there is a gentler and more natural way to be with horses but are struggling to find it. If you persevere and follow your heart and instincts, as Ellen did, then you will find the path that is right for you.

I recently found your article and signed up to have it sent to my email. I wanted to let you know how much I appreciate reading your answers to people's questions. They are written in a clear and compassionate way, and are somehow wonderfully encouraging to me as a horse person. I have been following your material in general for awhile. Before that, as someone who had never handled or ridden horses until age 40, I watched video tapes from Linda Tellington Jones (ground work) to teach myself how to interact with my recently acquired young horses. (Yes, I know, everybody but me says I did it the "wrong way around".)

The very small exposure I had to "conventional" horse handling was to later take some English riding lessons. It was enough to cause me to really shy away from what I saw was available out there and to continue my commitment to find alternative ways to interact with horses. The riding instructor had me hauling on the reins and squeezing with the legs to keep the horse in a frame. Very hard on my arms, my legs, and ultimately no sense of balance for me on the horse or movement with the horse's movement. But the big thing was that I could hardly bear to do that to the horse. It felt awful all the way around.

My inner sense of clear boundaries and respect probably enabled me to do so much (groundwork) with horses by myself and on my own. However, I mostly felt as though I was groping in the dark with what I was doing as I didn't have enough of a clear picture of how horses interact with each other and in their environment. In addition, I had a mountain of fear and self-doubt to work out with myself. The information you have been sharing (book, DVDs and the blog) has really helped me with confidence and has helped me to expand with clarity and energy to continue a wonderful exploration of relationship with horses. Thank you for offering written and filmed materials which been very inspiring to me!

I later had an opportunity to take a few riding lessons which were more in the style of "centered riding". I have ridden very infrequently because I have always wanted to feel more confidence and trust in relationship with horses before riding. This has been a very slowly evolving process! My hope is that you will continue with DVDs to follow from Panadero's Journey.

Virginia's Story

This is a story told to us by Virginia whose beloved horse has just passed away. The story she told touched me beyond words and I'd like to reproduce it here for you.

I awoke early this morning to read a small saying on the calendar, "We are shaped by what we love". We ended her pain today at 11:35 am (Sat. Feb. 2, 2008). Her feet don't have to hurt any more.

I flew home from San Diego last night and laid with her in the shavings in her stall. Then after she had fallen asleep, I went up to sit in the loft on a hay bale with my mom to look down onto her from above. We watched her blanket rise and fall with each breath. She was so peaceful in the stillness of that quiet night. I didn't want to go to sleep. I didn't know what the next day would bring being without her. I couldn't remember what life was like to exist without her.

I can remember the day I met her like it was just yesterday. My parents and I were looking for my first horse. I had begged for a year to have a horse and I had done everything my mother had told me I needed to do in order to prepare for such a time consuming pet. I had helped the other girls each day down at the barn with their horses and I had taken lessons to learn how to be safe around them and to ride. I didn't care what kind of horse or color, I just wanted one! We drove in the driveway to the farm where she lived. They had a beautiful home, barn and arena along with a wonderful Koi pond I admired. I remember walking into the barn with its golden brown wood stalls and black wrought iron bars. It seemed like you would have to be a special horse to live in this beautiful stall at such a fancy place.

As I walked down the aisle I saw her. She was standing on the crossties. She was beautiful. Her rich, brown color, her shiny coat and her soft kind eyes told me there was something special about her. She seemed to have a lot of spirit but she was so gentle and kind. They saddled her up and let me ride her around the arena. We got along great (though years later I would tell you that she was just a good "babysitter" as we called her, since her joy and purpose seemed to be keeping me safe and bringing me home in one piece, even if it was pitch black out). Then my mom and dad rode her, except my dad actually fell off, since he was more familiar with farm horses and she was a beautiful champion show horse! I just thought she was amazing and my parents seemed to agree with me (which was surprising due to my dads' first experience with her). I remember going back to the wash rack after our time with her and her owner showed me how to wash her off until the white water (sweat) wasn't coming off any more.

After much discussion, it was decided that we would buy her and they would deliver her the next week. I really just couldn't wait until she came home and I could brush her at the barn every day and pretty much spend every waking moment with her when I wasn't in school. And so that was the beginning - there were a lot of unforgettable years in the middle and now we have arrived at the end. Every day since I was seven years old she has been on my mind just as she was on her last day with me and I know she will still be every day after that. I now know the impact a 14.2 hand liver chestnut Morgan mare can have on my life and what an amazing journey it has been.

So now the last day was here. It was a beautiful morning. I awoke to a strange feeling in my stomach; something different than any other morning. It was to be my last morning with her. The sun had just come out as the fresh morning dew was drying up on the cool grass. I went straight to the barn to take her blanket off and let her out to walk in her favorite place, the back yard. It was quite crisp out but she was warm as she took time to rest and lay in the back yard, with the sun pushing through the clouds to warm her back. I braided her main and tail and for over an hour she wandered, eating grass and following me around. I gave her a couple of apples and she ate almost a loaf of bread (she loved bread). I figured she might as well go out with a full tummy. We spent the entire morning with her, the three of us. It seemed unusually silent as I brushed her (my parents sat in their chairs and video-taped me with her on the lawn). My dad sat with the syringe under his chair as if he was in no hurry to end this happy morning.

None of the other horses made a sound. The trees in the forest did not blow and I heard no birds chirping. At one point, she left the bite of bread in my hand and deliberately walked across the yard straight up to my mom and stood right in her face. My mom gave her a pet and thanked her for being such a good girl. Then she walked straight up to my dad. As if she was saying "thank you" to them. It was in that moment she knew; her demeanor quietened and she was comfortable with the decision. She went softly and slowly with her head in my lap and my mom and dad right next to her. I held her head in my hands and you could see she was at peace. No more pain, no more medicine, just peace. It truly couldn't have been a more beautiful morning and everything went as planned.

Just minutes after she laid down, the sun went behind the clouds and to this moment, it is still cloudy and grey out. She has truly shaped my life since I was seven years old. That quote means more than I could ever explain in words. She leaves behind her seven foals, a lifetime of Championships in the show ring and on the track as a trotter. She has travelled the U.S. and almost made it to 34 yrs old. She is a UVM Morgan born at the University of Vermont with amazing bloodlines, confirmation and a personality and trust that will never be reached by another in my eyes.

ABOUT CAROLYN RESNICK

Author of Naked Liberty and National Coach and Horse Trainer

Carolyn achieves a revolutionary connection between horses and humans on the ground and under saddle. She achieves this amazing connection through using the bonding rituals horses use to raise their young in a natural herd. Carolyn's lifelong passion for developing innovative horse training methods is based on an understanding of natural herd behavior that has evolved through many years of observing wild horses. Her observations led her to identify seven rituals that horses use to develop their language and social skills. She calls these rituals, when she uses them as a training method, the seven Waterhole Rituals™.

The Waterhole Rituals™ is truly unique as this is the only method of horse training that works with the horses' natural instincts and honors the right that the horse has the ability to make choices in whether he wants to follow your lead or not. The connection with horses that you gain from mastering the Waterhole Rituals™ translates across all equine disciplines making this Method the foundation for all equestrian pursuits. It can be used alongside any existing training method that you are currently working with. By communicating with horses using the Waterhole Rituals™ you can create a perfect connection on the ground that translates to a better performance under saddle. Through her program students gain a magnetic leadership ability working with horses in a free environment at liberty.

Carolyn's understanding of natural herd behavior, and the remarkable connection that she shares with all horses has spanned over 40 years as a trainer, Arabian breeder, clinician and student of wild horse behavior. Carolyn's life with horses began in Indio, California in the 1940s. Riding alone in the desert as a child she nurtured an intuitive bond with horses. As a junior rider she trained her own horses that she showed in both English and Western divisions wining many championships.

Carolyn was able to create a championship performance from the willing spirit of a horse gained from the natural connection she built with horses. She then went on to pursue a unique quest to gain more knowledge on natural wild horse behavior, pecking order, their communication systems and how lead horses go about creating a unified herd. She also studied families of horses and how mares raised their young and prepared them to be able to connect, communicate and fit in to a herd community. The knowledge that she gained from the study of natural herds brought more clarity in how to communicate with all horses around the world.

Today Carolyn trains large numbers of people all over the world in her Method through on-line coaching and hosts clinic at her ranch, Dance with Horses, in Escondido, California. For more information on Carolyn's work and to book a private clinic or purchase any of her products please visit www.CarolynResnickBlog.com or www.DancewithHorses.com